A Season of
Nature Poems for
Catholic Children

Autumn

An Autumn Season of Nature Poems for Catholic Children

Janet P. McKenzie, OCDS

A RACE for Heaven Book

Biblio Resource Publications, Inc.
108½ S. Moore St.
Bessemer, MI 49911
2020

OTHER BOOKS IN THE NATURE POEMS FOR CATHOLIC CHILDREN SERIES:

*A Winter Season of Nature Poems
for Catholic Children*

*A Spring Season of Nature Poems
for Catholic Children*

*A Summer Season of Nature Poems
for Catholic Children*

OTHER BOOKS BY JANET P. MCKENZIE

WWW.RACEFORHEAVEN.COM

STUDY GUIDES AND AIDS

✝ A Series of 20 Saint Study Guides for the saint books written by Mary Fabyan Windeatt (available as individual study guides or grade-level guides)

✝ *Graced Encounters with Mary Fabyan Windeatt's Saints: 344 Ways to Imitate the Holy Habits of Saints*

✝ *The Windeatt Dictionary: Pre-Vatican II Terms and Catholic Words from Mary Fabyan Windeatt's Saint Biographies*

✝ *Reading the Saints: Lists of Catholic Books for Children plus Book Collecting Tips for the Home and School Library, Second Edition*

✝ *Alternative Books Reports for Catholic Students*

✝ *The King of the Golden City Study Edition* (includes text and guide or individual guide available)

✝ *Outlaws of Ravenhurst Study Edition* (includes text and guide or individual guide available)

✝ *The Family that Overtook Christ Study Edition: Lessons in Sanctity from the Family of St. Bernard of Clairvaux* (includes text and guide)

✝ *By Cross and Anchor Study Edition: The Story of Frederic Baraga on Lake Superior* (includes text and guide)

RECONCILIATION/FIRST HOLY COMMUNION

✝ *A Reconciliation Reader-Retreat: Read-aloud Lessons, Stories, and Poems for Young Catholics Preparing for Confession*

- ✢ *Communion with the Saints, A Family Preparation Program for First Communion and Beyond in the Spirit of St. Therese*
- ✢ *The King of the Golden City Study Edition* (includes text and guide or individual guide available)
- ✢ *My First Communion Journal in Imitation of St. Therese, the Little Flower*
- ✢ *My First Communion Journal in Imitation of St. Paul: Putting on the Armor of God*
- ✢ *The Good Shepherd and His Little Lambs Study Edition: A First Communion Story-Primer*

SACRAMENT OF CONFIRMATION

- ✢ *A Confirmation Reader-Retreat: Read-Aloud Lessons, Stories, and Poems for Young Catholics*
- ✢ *The Family that Overtook Christ Study Edition: Lessons in Sanctity from the Family of St. Bernard of Clairvaux* (adult and teens)

ST. JOSEPH

- ✢ *The Month of St. Joseph: Prayers and Practices for Each Day of March in Imitation of the Virtues of St. Joseph* (adult)
- ✢ *Devotion to St. Joseph: Read-Aloud Stories, Poems, and Prayers for Catholic Children*

OTHER BOOKS

- ✢ *I Talk with God: The Art of Prayer and Meditation for Catholic Children*
- ✢ *Bedtime Bible Stories for Catholic Children: Loving Jesus through His Word*

THIS BOOK IS DEDICATED TO MY GRANDCHILDREN:
ALI, GRACE, NORAH, ETHAN, KATIE, JON, JACOB,
ELENA, AND ALL THOSE TO COME.

NATURE IS SO MUCH MORE FUN AND INSPIRING
WHEN I EXPLORE IT WITH YOU.

WITH GREAT LOVE,
NANA

ACKNOWLEDGEMENTS

Dust Jacket Design by Joshua Kodis

Dust Jacket Photo © lilkar
iStockPhoto.com

Dust Jacket Graphics ©lukpedclub
iStockPhoto.com

Divider Page Illustration ©logaryphmic
iStockPhoto.com

Illustration on September 5 ©AlexGreenArt
ShutterStock.com

Illustration on September 12 ©Taily
iStockPhoto.com

Illustration on October 5 ©Campwillowlake
iStockPhoto.com

Illustrations on October 16 and November 8
PublicDomainVectors.org

Illustration on November 3 © Kristisha07
iStockPhoto.com

But now ask the beasts to teach you,
the birds of the air to tell you;
Or speak to the earth to instruct you,
and the fish of the sea to inform you.
Which of all these does not know
that the hand of God has done this?

Job 12:7-9

And Nature, the old nurse, took
The child upon her knee,
Saying: "Here is a story-book
thy Father has written for thee."

"Come, wander with me," she said,
"Into regions yet untrod;
And read what is still unread
In the manuscripts of God."

And he wandered away and away
With Nature, the dear old nurse,
Who sang to him night and day
The rhymes of the universe.

From "The Fiftieth Birthday of Agassiz" by
Henry Wadsworth Longfellow (1807-1882)

TABLE OF CONTENTS

PREFACE

Throughout my childhood, my father worked as a manager in the Michigan State Parks system. We moved every three or four years to a different park within Michigan's Upper Peninsula. Even as a young child, I remember spending long days and evenings outdoors—in the woods, on the beach, in the yard. Many of these memories include my siblings and neighborhood friends. But many are the times I spent alone at various "secret" places I had found, places I often escaped to in order to think deep-child thoughts—to communicate with God.

Although I hesitate to compare my experiences with those of a saint, St. Thérèse the Little Flower, describes similar experiences in *The Story of a Soul*: "I preferred to go *alone* and sit down on the grass bedecked with flowers, and then my thoughts became very profound indeed! Without knowing what it was to meditate, my soul was absorbed in real prayer" (SOS 37). St. Thérèse talks often of how she was inspired to love, praise, and understand the God that the book of nature opened to her.

As a Discalced Carmelite Secular, my life is focused on union with God. Like St. Augustine (yes, another saint comparison!), I searched for many years for God, in various places and circumstances. However, in my Carmelite journey of faith, I have discovered that God can be found within. He resides in our very souls—nearer to us than we are to ourselves. Yet, in my adult searching, I have found —just as in my childhood—that I often commune best with Him in natural environments. I feel His presence in the beauty and holy silence of nature. Surrounded by creation, my mind frees, my soul fills with gratitude, and my heart connects with our loving Creator.

Preface

Here too we are in good company with the saints. Both St. Teresa of Jesus and St. John of the Cross, Carmelite Doctors, often used the natural world as a conduit to God:

✠ "It helped me also to look at fields, or water, or flowers. In these things I found a remembrance of the creator. I mean that they awakened and recollected me and served as a book and reminded me of my ingratitude and sins" (St. Teresa of Jesus, *Life* 9.5).

✠ "Beholding in creation a trace of the divine beauty, power, and loving wisdom, John could not easily resist the enchantment of nature. . . . He would take the friars out to the mountains . . . so that each might pass the day alone there 'in solitary prayer'" (*The Collected Works of St. John of the Cross* 26).

Many are the quotations we could cite from saints, popes, theologians, the Catechism, and Scripture that support an appreciation of the natural world as an important dimension of our relationship with God. However, we also need an awareness of the errors of the "New Age" movement, the theological problems with "nature worship", the heresy of pantheism, and an understanding that God does not depend upon creation for His identity to direct our path. If you are concerned or curious about these issues, please review the Appendix of this book.

In this series, we embark upon a study of nature and God in nature by reading aloud one poem per day, spending time daily outdoors, and, like St. Thérèse, thinking about God. I believe that the beauty, the rhythm, the flow, and the openness of poetry lends itself particularly useful as we journey closer to God with our beloved children and grandchildren in union with what Pope Frances calls "the joyful mystery of God" in creation. May God bless you!

16 July, 2019, Feast of Our Lady of Mount Carmel

A Few Explanations and Suggestions

The Purpose of This Study

The purpose of this poetical study of nature through the seasons is two-fold:

1) To seek and experience God personally and intimately by daily exposure to His creative work in nature

2) To better appreciate the connection between all of God's creation, its meaning and value, and its role—and ours—in the harmonious praise of God

Briefly, each creation of God has its own value and significance as well as a unique nature that is dependent on the rest of creation. Each creature works to complete and serve the rest of creation. (See *CCC* ¶340.) All of creation's natures, working together as a system of natures, are what we call "nature"—which "can only be understood as a gift from the outstretched hand of the Father of all" (*Laudato Si'* ¶76). The purpose of all of God's creation—including us—is to give Him praise and glory: ". . . so that we might exist for the praise of his glory . . ." (Ephesians 1:12).

Our study of God's creation through poetry and outdoor exploration is intended to allow children—and their adult companions—to experience God in a different way, to see Him in a new light, and to deepen our relationship and appreciation for Him and all of His creation—to learn to pray and praise God continuously. This is not a new way of experiencing God. Check out the Psalms and other books of the Bible. Refer to the writings of St. Thomas

1

Aquinas and many other saints. Peruse the teachings of our last three popes—St. Pope John Paul II, Pope Benedict XVI, and Pope Francis. Read through the *Catechism of the Catholic Church*, which clearly states: "There is a solidarity among all creatures arising from the fact that all have the same Creator and are all ordered to his glory . . ." (344). (For a more thorough treatment of seeking God through nature in accordance with the teachings of the Catholic Church, please see the Appendix of this book.)

Hopefully, through the gentle art of poetry and a daily commitment to experience God's creation outdoors, our relationship with God will become more awestruck as it becomes filled with the wonder, love, and appreciation of His divine wisdom and loving providence. God is more than willing to meet us whenever we reach out to Him. A little bit of openness and availability on our part will go a long way toward helping us fulfill our mission to praise God's glory in all our being. Let us begin today.

HOW THIS STUDY IS ORGANIZED

ASTRONOMICAL VS. METEOROLOGICAL SEASONS

Astronomical seasons are based on where the sun is in relation to the Earth, with the equinoxes (March and September) marking the dates where the day-to-night ratio is exactly twelve hours each. Because the Earth does not take exactly 365 days to travel around the sun, these dates vary but are generally considered to be March 21 and September 22 with the solstices usually falling on June 21 and December 22—the days with the longest and shortest periods of daylight. So the first day of each season according to the astronomical calendar would correspond to the varying dates of the spring and fall equinoxes and the summer and winter solstices.

The meteorological calendar for seasons uses the more general three-month chunk of time that is most closely associated with that season's weather. This calendar has the following seasonal dates:

- Winter: December 1 to February 28 or 29
- Spring: March 1 to May 31
- Summer: June 1 to August 31, and
- Autumn: September 1 to November 30

As the meteorological seasonal calendar corresponds more closely with our liturgical year, which begins in the season of Advent around December 1, (and breaks the months of each season more cleanly), this poetical study of the seasons uses the meteorological calendar to track the seasons.

(Please note that much of the material in this study is geared toward the weather and activities common to the temperate climates. My personal experience is almost exclusively that of the upper Midwest of the United States. Adaptation may be necessary depending on your location.)

LITURGICAL VS. NATURAL YEAR

Traditionally, we Americans often begin new projects and make new resolutions at the beginning of our Gregorian calendar year on January 1. Our Church's Roman Rite liturgical new year always begins on the first Sunday of Advent. This date is determined by when the Sunday closest to the Feast of St. Andrew (November 30) falls. The earliest this date can be is November 27, and the latest possible date is December 3. The beginning of the winter season of this series would roughly correspond with the beginning of the Church's liturgical new year.

The other major season of the liturgical year is the season of Lent, which is generally associated with the natural

3

season of spring. As the timing of this season depends on the moveable feast day of Easter, Ash Wednesday, the first day of Lent, may be as early as February 4 or as late as March 10, with the date of Easter itself ranging from March 22 to April 25. Therefore, the Lenten season is covered in this study in both the winter and spring seasons.

WHEN AND HOW TO START

There is no "right" starting place for this series—no "correct" season to begin this poetical study of God's creation. Many may wish to start with the Church's new liturgical year in December—the winter season. However, feel free to start with the season that best suits your own calendar and availability. Perhaps summer, when school is in recess and life is more laid back, is a better fit for your schedule. Quite possibly, autumn— the beginning of the school year—appeals to you as the best time to start. Maybe you want to examine the optional theme for each season and choose to begin according to which theme seems most interesting to you and your family.

Whenever you begin, remember the program's two main rules:

1. Read one poem daily *aloud* and have a short discussion on it. (Suggestions for age-appropriate questions can be found below.)
2. Spend at least thirty minutes each and every day outdoors, exploring God's beautiful creative work. This includes you as well as the children. Always keep in mind that the best way to get children outdoors is to go with them. Trust me; you will be enriched beyond your expectations. Do not hesitate to assume the role of nature mentor to help

your children or grandchildren increase their love of nature and deepen their experience of God. Review the section on nature mentoring if you need the reassurance that no prior experience or knowledge is necessary. You—yes, you—can do this!

THE DAILY ROUTINE

THE POEMS – DAILY AND SUPPLEMENTAL

For each day of the year, a poem (or several shorter poems) is presented for reading. The poem may be about an aspect of nature for that season, relate to the seasonal theme, or to a specific activity common for that season. Read each poem aloud. Perhaps each child could also read the poem aloud. Read slowly and with feeling. Don't hesitate to re-read the poem several times. If a child takes a special liking to a poem, help the child to memorize it. Having three or four favorite poems in a memory bank provides a store of great pleasure that will bubble up and spill out on days when our love of nature overwhelms us and we have no other way to express our joy in that special experience. It is a great treasure.

In addition to the daily poems, several other poems are available in the supplemental poetry section following the daily poems. These poems focus on the liturgical year or specific national holidays. They may be chosen to read aloud instead of, or in addition to, the poem for each day. There is a poem available for each day of Christmas, each day of Lent, and at least one poem for each significant holiday or Catholic holy day. Additionally, there are poems for meditation upon the themes for the First Friday and First Saturday devotions. Use the supplemental poems as you deem best for your family— either replacing the daily poem, read in addition to the daily poem, or not read at all. If you wish to incorporate them into the daily routine, it may require some preparation time to preview these poems to determine which ones best suit your family and purposes. Be sure to discuss these poems with the children/grandchildren just as you would the daily poems.

As you and your family begin to read more and more poetry, be sure to note favorite poets. Go online and check out more poems by these favorites or perhaps purchase as a gift an entire volume written by them. Pay attention to the type of poetry (rhythm and rhyme scheme) that appeals to each child. Encourage them to take a favorite poem, study how it is written, and use it as a pattern for writing an original poem of their own. Perhaps after reading a poem, they may decide that they could write a better poem on that topic. The world needs poetry and poets; coax the young poets around you to produce poetry that they enjoy writing and sharing. Model writing poetry by generating poems of your own.

DISCUSSION

To encourage discussion, always ask open-ended questions that require more than a yes/no answer. For younger children, the following questions offer a good beginning but remember that not all questions will apply to every poem. As you gain confidence, feel free to construct your own questions geared toward the ages and interests of your own children/grandchildren.

1. What is this poem about?
2. How does this poem make you feel?
3. What action do you want to take because of this poem?
4. What did you learn from this poem?
3. What does this poem suggest about God?

A different approach is to ask each child to retell the poem in their own words, starting with the youngest child and having each child add something to the retelling. (Educator Charlotte Mason calls this technique "narration.")

For older children (and adults), try using the following three principles/realities/values that stem from the teachings of Thomas Berry, Catholic eco-theologian and author of several books including *The Dream of the Earth* and *The Great Work: Our Way into the Future*. According to Thomas Berry, these three characteristics govern the universe and reveal what the universe has to teach us. (These questions are also appropriate to ask as a nature mentor when outside exploring nature with children.)

1. Uniqueness (Each creation offers a unique expression of the divine, an authenticity that illustrates how the divine image dwells within.)
   - How is this creation different from all others? What makes it unique?
   - How does it reveal the divine?

2. Interior Identity
   - What is the job or specific task of this creation?
   - How does it function?
   - How does it give harmonious praise to God?

3. Communion/Connection
   - What is the relationship between this creation and the rest of creation?
   - How does it serve or provide for the rest of creation?
   - How is it connected to or dependent upon the rest of creation?

The Quotations

The quotations beneath the daily poems are included for the adults participating in this study. Often, as we feed our children the knowledge and inspiration they crave and need, our own needs may go unfulfilled. These short selections are intended to inspire you, deepen your understanding about an idea or topic, or add a touch of humor.

Additional Resources

This section first includes appropriate picture books for children. In preparation for this section, hundreds of possibly worthy picture books were read and examined; many of these books were discarded in favor of the exceptional books chosen for each season. The books marked "Stellar" would be considered "must reads" for each season. The remaining books have been categorized according to the holidays and optional themes for each season. The intention is that these books would be read aloud by either an adult or child.

Depending on the interests of your children/grandchildren, you may wish to focus on one particular theme or perhaps choose several books from each category. (It would be hard to read them all!) As you read through these books, be sure to note the author of those books you particularly enjoy. Watch for other books by these authors listed in this series, and/or check them out at your local library.

After the final section of picture books, there is a short section on other nature books for children. This section varies with the season and is outlined below.

Fall: A Short List of Children's Nature Chapter Books
Winter: Nature Non-fiction Books for Children
Spring: A Short List of Children's Nature Authors

Summer: A Short List of Children's Nature Poets, Collectable Children's Poetry Books, and A Few Children's Poetry Anthologies

The last part of this section contains recommended adult books that fall loosely in the following categories:

- The "Why" of Nature
- Connection with Nature
- Nature Activity Books—Outdoor Adventuring
- Nature Journaling
- Nature Crafts and Drawing Books
- Nature Books for Grandparents
- The Practice of *Shinrin-yoku:* Forest Therapy or Forest Bathing
- The Practice of Mindfulness

OUTSIDE ACTIVITY

The crux and primary purpose of this poetry series is to explore nature and to seek God in His beautiful creation. If you are unsure about what to do outside, check out the "Additional Resources" section described above for ideas. Assume your role as nature mentor as described on pages 17-21 below.

By spending unfettered time in nature, we will unleash our sense of wonder and come to better understand God. By increasing our familiarity with different aspects of nature, we will begin to see the connection between all creation and discover the loving concern God has for His creation.

Please make the effort to get your family (including yourself!) outside for least thirty minutes each day—an hour would not be too much! Get outside, play, experience creation, and live in the present moment. Be sure to pause occasionally in holy silence to give thanks, glory, and praise to our awesome Creator!

OPTIONAL SEASONAL THEMES

For those interested in a more guided study of nature, each season has a theme of recommended focus. These themes provide a hub around which outside activity for each season can be centered as well as an emphasis on specific knowledge and experience of God's created world.

Do not get obsessive with the suggested resources below. Choose only those best suited to your particular situation. Be flexible. Taylor these suggestions to your own circumstances and time allowances.

AUTUMN THEME: Respecting God's Creation through Care of the Natural World

- GOAL: Eco-Catholic

- DEFINITION OF ECO-CATHOLIC: Someone who values not only Catholic spirituality and doctrine but also the natural world, the environment, and justice

- SUMMARY: In his 2015 encyclical *Laudato Si'*, Pope Francis encourages "every person living on this planet" to take better care of our common home, Earth. Like his three predecessors, he emphasizes the need to care for and understand the connection between all of God's creation. Review carefully your family's relationship with the natural world and the habits that support the environment and those that are detrimental. "Care for the environment represents a challenge for all of humanity. It is a matter of a common and universal duty, that of respecting a common good" (Pope St. John Paul II, *Centesimus Annus*, 40).

- ADULT RESOURCES
  - *Caring for Creation in Your Own Backyard: Over 100 Things Christian Families Can Do to Help the Earth (A Seasonal Guide)* by Loren & Mary Ruth Wilkinson
  - *Earthsongs: Praying with Nature* by Wayne Simsic
  - *In Defense of Nature* by Benjamin Wiker
  - *Laudato Si'* by Pope Francis
  - *Life from Our Land* by Marcus Grodi
  - *The Joyful Mystery: Field Notes toward a Green Thomism* by Christopher J. Thompson

- CHILDREN'S RESOURCES
  - *Celebrate the Earth: Psalm 104* by Dorrie Papademetriou
  - *Crinkleroot's Guide to Giving Back to Nature* by Jim Arnosky
  - *Song of Francis* by Tomie dePaola
  - Read and implement actions proposed by Pope Francis in ¶211 of *Laudato Si'*.

WINTER THEME: Reflecting on the Mystery of God through Natural Prayer

- DEFINITION OF NATURAL PRAYER: Finding intimacy with God by experiencing Him in the beauty of nature; prayer experienced amidst creation (Beware, however, of the caution expressed by St. John of the Cross in *Ascent of Mount Carmel* 3.24.4: If the heart and soul are not elevated to God, an experience of sensory delight may merely be another form of recreation.)

- GOAL: Mystic—someone who seeks union with God through prayer and self-surrender

- SUMMARY: The season of winter—when much of nature is at rest and we anticipate and contemplate the Mystery of God in the Christ Child—is a great time to reconnect with that wonder for God that natural experiences (a beautiful sunset, a snowy-topped mountain, a perfect snowflake) so easily enkindle. Enjoy the stillness of winter while practicing the virtue of holy silence—quiet walks in the snow, a pause to listen to the winter birds. Take your daily prayer time (rosary or meditation) outside. "We need to find God, and he cannot be found in noise and restlessness. God is the friend of silence. See how nature—trees, flowers, grass—grows in silence; see the stars, the moon and the sun, how they move in silence . . ." (St. Teresa of Calcutta).

- ADULT RESOURCES
    - 📖 *Natural Prayer: Encountering God in Nature* by Wayne Simsic
    - 📖 *The Secret Life of John Paul II* by Lino Zani
    - 📖 *When the Trees Say Nothing* by Thomas Merton

- CHILDREN'S RESOURCES
    - 📖 *A Quiet Place* by Douglas Wood
    - 📖 *Crinkleroot's Book of Animal Tracking* by Jim Arnosky
    - 📖 *The Other Way to Listen* by Byrd Baylor
    - 📖 *The Wild Weather Book* by Fiona Danks and Jo Schofield
    - 📖 *WoodsWalk* by Henry W. Art and Michael W. Robbins

SPRING THEME: Detecting God in Nature through Phenology

- DEFINITION OF PHENOLOGY: Nature's calendar; nature's clock; the study of the timing of seasonal biological activities including first flowers, leaf budding, bird migration, etc. (We can also include *seasonality*, which is the study of changes in the physical environment such as first frost, date the ice melts, etc.)

- GOAL: Nature Detective—someone who carefully observes the wonders and mystery of nature

- SUMMARY: Spend spring observing firsts and lasts in nature: first robin, first eruptions of various plants and flowers, first sound of the frog voices, last frost, last ice on the lake. Mark these dates on a regular or perpetual calendar—an excellent beginning toward keeping a more complete nature journal. Allow the children free rein to explore and take notes and photos of various aspects of God's creation. "Nature is a constant source of wonder and awe" (Pope Francis, *Laudato Si'* 85).

- ADULT RESOURCES
  - 📖 Daily readings from any of the following: *Hal Borland's Book of Days* (New England), *A Walk through the Year* by Edwin Way Teale (New England), or *Wit & Wisdom of the Great Out-doors* by Larry Wilber (upper Midwest)
  - 📖 **Or** weekly readings from *The Beginning Naturalist* by Gale Lawrence or shorter articles for each month in *A Seasonal Guide to the Natural Year* by John Bates

13

(upper Midwest), or *Minnesota Phenology* by Larry Weber

📖 **Or** browse through any calendar/almanac suited to your location.

📖 Check into joining a citizen science program of interest.

- CHILDREN'S RESOURCES
  - 📖 *Crinkleroot's Nature Almanac* by Jim Arnosky
  - 📖 *One Day in the Woods* by Jean Craighead George
  - 📖 *This World of Wonder* by Hal Borland
  - 📖 *When I Consider* by Marian M. Schoolland

SUMMER THEME: Inspecting God's Glorious Creation through Naming Nature (Nomenclature)

- DEFINITION OF NOMENCLATURE: A system of names in a given field such as botany or biology

- GOAL: Naturalist—someone who is an expert or student in the study of plants, animals, and the natural world

- SUMMARY: By taking an interest in nature and being willing to make the acquaintance of the most common natural elements in your locale—by learning the names of the most common birds, flowers, and trees—we can become more acquainted with all that surrounds us in God's great outdoors. Names foster familiarity, and lead to a sense of connection. "What I know of the divine sciences and the Holy Scriptures, I have learned in woods and fields. I have no other masters than the beeches and the oaks" (St. Bernard of Clairvaux).

- ADULT RESOURCES
    - 📖 *Beyond Your Doorstep* by Hal Borland
    - 📖 *Circle of the Seasons* by Edwin Way Teale
    - 📖 *Exploring Nature with Your Child* by Dorothy Edwards Shuttlesworth
    - 📖 *Great Lakes Nature* by Mary Blocksma
    - 📖 *Handbook of Nature Study* by Anna Botsford Comstock [a classic since 1939]
    - 📖 *The Naturalist's Notebook* by Nathaniel T. Wheelwright and Bernd Heinrich
- CHILDREN'S RESOURCES
    - 📖 Regional field guides (the more specific to your area the better) to birds, flowers, insects, trees, or any other area of interest
    - 📖 *Nature Anatomy* by Julia Rothman
    - 📖 Any of the *True Books* (*True Book of Insects*, etc.) published by Children's Press in the 1950's and 1960's
    - 📖 Any of Jim Arnosky's *Crinkleroot's Guide to Knowing* books (*Birds, Trees,* etc.)
    - 📖 *Crinkleroot's Guide to Walking in Wild Places*

———

Note that these suggested themes are *optional*. If the children are young, or if the themes seem intimidating to implement, feel free to skip them. Perhaps you would like to utilize the picture books as your only use of the optional season themes. Or maybe you would like to study the suggested adult resources for your own enrichment without adding the children's resources.

Be kind to yourself. We're going for joy here—not added stress! Do not put pressure to use every resource and/or theme. Attach no guilt to customizing and simplifying. The main objective is to enjoy God's creation and to connect with the Creator—not to cram in every possible teaching moment. Allow the children to ask and find answers to their own spontaneous questions in an adventure of discovery at their own lead. Relax and enjoy!

"FOR FROM THE GREATNESS
AND THE BEAUTY OF CREATED THINGS
THEIR ORIGINAL AUTHOR,
BY ANALOGY, IS SEEN."

WISDOM 13:5

YOU CAN BECOME A NATURE MENTOR
(ALMOST WITHOUT TRYING)

"If a child is to keep alive his inborn sense of wonder . . . he needs the companionship of at least one adult who can share it, rediscovering with him the joy, excitement, and mystery of the world we live in" (Rachel Carson in *A Sense of Wonder*). This "one adult" becomes this child's nature mentor. It is not a difficult task. It does not require vast knowledge. According to Rachel Carson, it is based upon "having fun together rather than teaching." Whether you are a grandparent, a parent, a teacher, the neighbor down the street, or an aunt like Rachel Carson, you need no advance preparation other than asking yourself, "Am I up for adventure?" "Can I handle being a co-conspirator?"

The best nature mentors are not those who have the answers but who can stimulate the questions, who can step aside and let the child take charge. Effective nature mentors are those who are fellow adventurers, willing to let their own sense of wonder come alive, and share their feelings about nature—and reverence for nature—rather than merely providing explanations and facts. Observe and explore. Be aware and listen—not only to the wonders around you but to those sharing the experience with you. Be respectful to the child's interests and enthusiasms. Be attentive to the present moment—the activity and the feelings that are evoked.

Ask questions. Point out interesting sights, sounds, animals, and plants. Bring home specimens to talk about, learn about, and display. Include God in the discussion.

Help them to observe the activity around them. Allow them to directly experience the wonder that surrounds them —saving the "teaching moment" for a later recap of the event. Encourage them to see, hear, smell, and touch. Allow them not only to run and enjoy but also to sit in holy silence and observe—watch the grass bending in the wind, hear the babble of nearby water and birds, smell the flowers and the bark of the trees, touch the moss and slippery rocks—pondering and raising the heart to God. The love of nature is best inspired by experiencing nature —even quiet observation can be an interactive encounter on an emotional level.

Be enthusiastic and joyful in all their discoveries. Play games; join in their fun. Often, the memory of an experience is associated with the emotions related to that experience. By making time with nature joy-filled, joy will come to be an emotion associated with nature itself.

Sharing the natural world with others adds to the richness of the encounter—not only at the moment but later in discussion. Take time each day to reflect together on time spent in nature, reviewing individual discoveries and emotions. In this way, everyone benefits from each person's experience and insights, and our own encounters become more meaningful. Additionally, a bit of nature bonding and affirmation occurs that binds us with each other, and more deeply with the created world.

As a nature mentor, basic knowledge may be helpful but, in this case, only a little knowledge of nature is not a dangerous thing—or even detrimental. Enjoyment of simple natural aspects (the colors of the sunset, the blowing clouds, the calls of birds, the vastness of the night sky, the feel of rain on your face) will serve to enkindle more joy and wonder than many interesting facts. "I sincerely believe that for the child, and for the parent seeking to guide him, it is not half so important to know as to feel" (Rachel Carson).

It is more helpful to arouse their curiosity and sense of wonder than to pepper them with facts and names they may or may not be able to assimilate. As a nature mentor, receptivity and awareness trump personal resources. Is it less wondrous to gaze at the night sky even if you do not know the name of a single star or constellation?

Encourage exploration using the senses of smell and hearing. This is particularly effective at night and in rainy weather. The smell of the ocean, frog ponds, and rain-filled forests can provide lasting memories. The night sound of insects, frogs, flight of birds overhead, thunder, and wind are especially powerful. Try to focus not only on the full chorus of sound but also on each of the individual contributors. Seek where they are hiding.

Unfortunately, it is easy to become immune to the wonder of God's creation—to become insensitive to repeated exposure to God's great gifts. Rachel Carson would have us ask, "What if I had never seen this before? What if I knew I would never see it again?" Like the reception of Holy Communion, when we take for granted that we can receive It often, we often receive It less (and less reverently). The same holds true of God's gifts within the natural world. Because we can see it all the time, we often see (and enjoy its benefits) less often. When is the last time you took the time to explore the night sky? Or pause your busy agenda to enjoy the glorious sunset? Or listen attentively for even a minute or two to the morning chorus of birds? Learn to tune in to God not only in church, but also in His cathedral of the natural world.

RESOURCES

So what resources are required to be an effective nature mentor? For starters, you may want to read one or more of the books that most directly influenced the above insights and ideas:

📖 *The Sense of Wonder* by Rachel Carson (1956)

📖 *Sharing Nature with Children: The Classic Parents' and Teachers' Nature Awareness Guidebook* by Joseph Cornell (1979—a newer edition is available)

📖 *How to Raise a Wild Child: The Art and Science of Falling in Love with Nature* by Scott D. Sampson (2015)

Spending a few dollars on a good magnifying glass or hands lens will pay off handsomely. With this, a snowflake or grain of sand takes on far greater wonder as does a drop of pond water or the moon at night. You may wish to throw down another couple of dollars on child-sized flashlights—or ultraviolet flashlights!—for night exploration of insects, rocks, and flowers. (Bedtime can wait!)

As far as expensive equipment and toys, do not let your heart be troubled. In 2012, *Wired* magazine published an article entitled "The 5 Best Toys of All Time." Here is your shopping list:

1. Stick
2. Box
3. String
4. Cardboard Tube
5. Dirt

If you must spend money, a few good field guides may be helpful—the more regional the better—for identification of common trees, birds, flowers, and insects. Keep in mind, however, this caution from Rachel Carson: "I think the value of the game of identification depends on how you play it. If it becomes an end in itself, I count it of little use. It is possible to compile extensive lists of creatures seen and identified without ever once having caught a breath-taking glimpse of the wonder of life. If a child asked me a question that suggested even a faint awareness of the mystery behind the arrival of a migrant sandpiper on the beach of an August morning, I would be far more pleased than by the mere fact that he knew it was a sandpiper and not a plover."

A pair of puddle boots, some old clothes, and raingear (purchased or makeshift) will allow your child to explore without fear of "getting dirty." Be sure to provide the same for yourself.

Nature mentoring really is as simple as accompanying kids outside and letting them do what comes naturally. Let them be the boss. If you are doubtful, try at least a half-hour outside every day for a month—put it on your calendar. While Scott Sampson in *How to Raise a Wild Child* claims, "The best place to fall in love with nature is wherever you happen to be," be sure to vary the setting occasionally. Find a place where you (as well as the children) are excited to be. See what effect this daily thirty-minute habit has—on you and the kids!

Rachel Carson had one wish for every child: ". . . a sense of wonder so indestructible that it would last throughout life, as an unfailing antidote against the boredom and disenchantments of later years, the sterile preoccupation with things that are artificial, the alienation from the sources of our strength." It is in wonder that we often find God.

> "...HE FIXED THE ORDERED SEASONS
> AND THE BOUNDARIES OF
> THEIR REGIONS,
> SO THAT PEOPLE MIGHT SEEK GOD,
> EVEN PERHAPS GROPE FOR HIM
> AND FIND HIM,
> THOUGH INDEED HE IS NOT FAR
> FROM ANY ONE OF US."
>
> ACTS 17:26-27

SEPTEMBER

I LIKE TO WANDER OFF ALONE

Annette Wynne (died 1953), published in
For Days and Days, 1919

I like to wander off alone
And climb upon a great tall stone,
And wonder.

I like to wonder at the sky,
The curly cloud that tumbles by;
I like to wonder at the grass
And all the flying things that pass,
I wonder if they wonder, too.
The little things—perhaps they do,
Perhaps they wonder who am I
To stare at them as they pass by;

The curly cloud looks down at me
And wonders, too, what I may be,
A tiny spot, so very small.
The cloud can hardly see at all;
And all the world is wondering
At every other wondering thing,
There's so much wondering to do,
I wonder if I could get through;

I think perhaps I might some day
If I should never stop for play—
I wonder!

"THE LORD GOD THEN TOOK THE MAN AND SETTLED HIM IN THE GARDEN OF EDEN, TO CULTIVATE AND CARE FOR IT." – GENESIS 2:15

September 1
World Day of Prayer for the Care of Creation

PROVERB
Cree Indian Proverb

Only when the last tree has died

And the last river has been poisoned
And the last fish has been caught
Will we realize that we cannot eat money.

RARE SEPTEMBER
Published in *Child's Calendar Beautiful*, 1905

'Tis the radiant rare September,

With the clusters ripe on the vine.
With scents that mingle in spicy tingle
On the hill slope's glimmering line.

And summer's a step behind us,
And autumn's a thought before,
And each fleet sweet day that we meet on the
way
Is an angel at the door.

"Rather than a problem to be solved, the world is a
joyful mystery to be contemplated with gladness and
praise." – *Laudato Si'* 12

SEPTEMBER

Helen Hunt Jackson (1830-1885), published in
"Teacher's Magazine", Volume 36, 1913

The golden-rod is yellow;
The corn is turning brown;
The trees in apple orchards
With fruit are bending down.
The gentian's bluest fringes
Are curling in the sun;
In dusty pods the milkweed
Its hidden silk has spun.
The sedges flaunt their harvest,
In every meadow nook;
And asters by the brook-side
Make asters in the brook,
From dewy lanes at morning
The grapes' sweet odors rise;
At noon the roads all flutter
With yellow butterflies.
By all these lovely tokens
September days are here,
With summer's best of weather,
And autumn's best of cheer. . . .

"To learn something new, take the path that you took
yesterday." – John Burroughs

ST. GREGORY THE GREAT
Robert Hugh Benson (1871-1914), published in
An Alphabet of Saints, 1906

"G" is for GREGORY the GREAT, who
walked about the town
Of Rome, and found the English slaves on sale
for half-a-crown;
"Why have these boys blue eyes," he asked,
"when ours have eyes of brown?"
When he heard that they were Angles, and
that Allah was their king,
He said, "In the land of Allah, 'Alleluia' they
shall sing;
For we'll make the Angles Angels by the
message that we'll bring."
St. AUGUSTINE went to Angleland for Pope
Saint GREGORY,
And converted our poor ancestors to Christianity;
And that is why both you and I are Christians,
don't you see?

(ST. GREGORY the GREAT, Pope, Confessor, Doctor of
the Church; Born in Rome, 540; Pope 590-604. Feast,
September 3)

"'The external deserts in the world are growing,
because the internal deserts have become so
vast.' For this reason, the ecological crisis is also a
summons to profound interior conversion."
Laudato Si' 217

GOD'S HOUSE HAS A CEILING
Annette Wynne (died 1953), published in
For Days and Days, 1919

God's house has a ceiling that's curved and far
and high,
And beautiful and soft and blue—God's ceiling is
the sky.
And from God's ceiling hang rare lamps all radiant
with light,
One great big sun for all the day, and a million
stars for night.

NUTS
A Folk Tale

The leaves are green, the nuts are brown,
They hang so high they'll not come down.
Leave them alone till frosty weather,
Then they will all come down together.

"The sky is that beautiful old parchment in which the
sun and the moon keep their diary."
Alfred Kreymborg

THE SUNFLOWER'S LESSON
Published in *Catholic National Series,*
Third Reader, 1891

A nice little sunflower, just over the way,

Is blooming four inches tall, I should say,
And what is the reason it blossoms so low?
Has bright little Sunflower forgotten to grow?

Oh, no! But the season is getting quite late;
The frosts will be coming, and so it can't wait.
It seems to be saying, the sunflower so small,
Better blossom thus low than not at all!

The lesson I read in the sunflower's face:
To fill well a low place is not a disgrace.
Make the most of your time, and your talents
  though small:
Better bloom in low place than not bloom at all.

"The Lord was instructing her [St. Therese of Lisieux]
through 'Nature's own book.' Therese delighted in
these lessons." – Conrad de Meester,
With Empty Hands

FAREWELL, SUMMER

Abbie Farwell Brown (1871-1927), published in
Songs of Sixpence, 1914

Fare you well, sweet summer playtime,
   Happy days amid the flowers.
Fare you well, dear summer daytime,
   Azure skies and golden hours.
All the pleasant haunts that knew me,
   All the trees that bent above,
Summer scents and sounds that drew me
   To the Nature that I love.

Will my flower friends betray me?
   Will the whispering pines forget,
In whose shade I long to lay me?—
   Comrades brave, I see you yet!
Will the brook I loved to follow
   Drown my memory in the sea?
Will the veery and the swallow
   Sing and soar, forgetting me?

Fare you well, sweet summer playtime,
   Happy life amid the flowers.
Fare you well, dear summer daytime.
   Azure skies and golden hours.

"There [among the trees] I sat in silence and loved the wind in the forest and listened for a good while to God." – Thomas Merton, *When the Trees Say Nothing*

SEPTEMBER (FROM)

Mary Howitt (1799-1888), published in
Poetry for the Young: A Collection, 1884

There are twelve months throughout the year,
From January to December—
And the primest month of all the twelve
Is the merry month of September!
Then apples so red
Hang overhead,
And nuts ripe-brown
Come showering down
In the bountiful days of September!

There are flowers enough in the summer-time,
More flowers than I can remember—
But none with the purple, gold, and red
That dye the flowers of September!
The gorgeous flowers of September!
And the sun looks through
A clearer blue,
And the moon at night
Sheds a clearer light
On the beautiful flowers of September!

"Everything in creation—be it a star or a flower—is a
sign that, if followed, leads to God."
Christopher West, *Theology of the Body*

September 8
Nativity of the Blessed Virgin Mary

MARY'S BIRTHDAY

Sister Mary Josita Belger (1899-1978), published in
Sing a Song of Holy Things, 1945

This is our Mother's birthday;
Let's visit her today,
Place lights upon her altar,
And flowers bright and gay.

But more than that, let's sing our love
And whisper soft prayers, too.
Then she will take each little child
Under her mantle blue.

Mary dear, look down, we pray,
From your bright, shining throne.
Tell Jesus all about us;
Help us live for Him alone.

Mother and maiden,
Was never none but she!
Well might such a lady
God's mother be. – Old Carol

THE NEWS
Persis Gardnier, published in
School Education, Volume 23, 1904

The katydid says it as plain as can be,
And the crickets are singing it under the tree;
In the aster's blue eyes you may read the same
 hint,
Just as clearly as if you had seen it in print;
And the corn sighs it, too, as it waves in the sun,
That autumn is here; and summer is done.

"The pastures are clothed with flocks,
the valleys blanketed with grain;
they cheer and sing for joy." – Psalms 65:14

MAPLE SEEDS

Kate Louise Brown (1837-1921), published in
The Plant Baby and Its Friends, 1897

U nder the green leaves
Somebody swings,
Stretching and straining
Two little wings.

"Wait," pleads the mother tree,
Coaxing and mild,
"You must not leave me,
Rash little child!"

Under the red leaves
Somebody swings;
Stout is the little heart.
Strong are the wings.

"Come!" shouts the trumpet wind,
"Cold days are nigh."
Cheerily calls he,
"Mother, good-by!"

Brave little maple-seed
Soars to the sky.

"I believe in the forest, and in the meadow, and in
the night in which the corn grows."
Henry David Thoreau

AUTUMN
Emily Dickinson (1830-1886),
published in *Poems*, 1890

The morns are meeker than they were,

The nuts are getting brown;
The berry's cheek is plumper,
The rose is out of town.

The maple wears a gayer scarf,
The field a scarlet gown.
Lest I should be old-fashioned,
I'll put a trinket on.

AUTUMN
Florence Hoatson (1881-1964), published in
The Little White Gate, 1925

Yellow the bracken,

Golden the sheaves.
Rosy the apples,
Crimson the leaves.
Mist on the hillside,
Clouds grey and white.
Autumn, good morning!
Summer, good night!

"Joys come from simple and natural things; mist over
meadows, sunlight on leaves, the path of the moon
over water. Even rain and wind and stormy clouds
bring joy." — Sigurd F. Olson

I Meant to Do My Work Today
Richard Le Gallienne (1866-1947),
published in *The Melody of Earth*, 1918

I meant to do my work today

But a brown bird sang in the apple-tree,
And a butterfly flitted across the field,
And all the leaves were calling me.

And the wind went sighing over the land,
Tossing the grasses to and fro.
And a rainbow held out its shining hand
So what could I do but laugh and go?

"When we can see God reflected in all that exists, our
hearts are moved to praise the Lord for all his
creatures and to worship him in union with them."
Laudato Si' 87

GOLDEN-ROD

Frank Dempster Sherman (1860-1916), published in
The Poems of Frank Dempster Sherman, 1887

Spring is the morning of the year,
And summer is the noontide bright;
The autumn is the evening clear
That comes before the winter's night.

And in the evening, everywhere
Along the roadside, up and down,
I see the golden torches flare
Like lighted streetlamps in the town.

I think the butterfly and bee,
From distant meadows coming back,
Are quite contented when they see
These lamps along the homeward track.

But those who stay too late get lost;
For when the darkness falls about,
Down every lighted street the Frost
Will go and put the torches out.

"It is our humble conviction that the divine and the
human meet in the slightest detail in the seamless
garment of God's creation, in the last speck of dust of
our planet." – *Laudato Si'* 9

THERE WAS NO ROOM ON THE CROSS
Published in
The Golden Book of Catholic Poetry, 1946

I thought that I could follow Him;
But when my feet drew near
To Calvary, at dead of night,
I quailed in utter fear.

Whereat a voice came whispering,
Through darkness, like a sea:
"Child, child, be not afraid. Your Cross
Is occupied by Me."

THE KNIGHT OF BETHLEHEM
Henry Neville Maugham (1868-1904), published in *Yuletide Cheer: A Book of Verses for the Christmas Season*, 1912

There was a Knight of Bethlehem
Whose wealth was tears and sorrows;
His men-at-arms were little lambs,
His trumpeters were sparrows.
His castle was a wooden cross,
On which He hung so high;
His helmet was a crown of thorns,
Whose crest did reach the sky.

"Saint John of the Cross taught that all the goodness
present in the realities and experiences of this world 'is
present in God eminently and infinitely, or more
properly, in each of these sublime realities is God.' . . .
the mystic experiences the intimate connection
between God and all beings . . ." – *Laudato Si'* 234

OUR LORD AND OUR LADY

Hilaire Belloc (1870-1953), published in *Verses*, 1910

They warned our Lady for the Child
That was our blessed Lord,
And she took Him into the desert wild,
Over the camel's ford.

And a long song she sang to Him
And a short story told;
And she wrapped Him in a woolen cloak
To keep Him from the cold.

But when our Lord was grown a man
The rich they dragged Him down,
And they crucified Him in Golgotha,
Out and beyond the town.

They crucified Him on Calvary,
Upon an April day;
And because He had been her little Son
She followed Him all the way.

Our Lady stood beside the Cross,
A little space apart,
And when she heard our Lord cry out
A sword went through her heart.

They laid our Lord in a marble tomb,
Dead, in a winding sheet.
But our Lady stands above the world
With the white moon at her feet.

"The Father is the ultimate source of everything . . .
The Son . . . united himself to this earth when he was
formed in the womb of Mary. The Spirit . . . is intimately
present at the very heart of the universe . . . Consequently, 'when we contemplate with wonder the
universe in all its grandeur and beauty, we must
praise the whole Trinity.'" – *Laudato Si'* 238

September 16

LOOK AND LISTEN
Published in *Poems for Memorization*, 1988

Look and listen! Autumn's here.
Hills are hazy, skies are clear.
Birds are leaving, southward bound.
Goldenrod in bloom is found.
Brittle cornstalks and crisp leaves
Rustle in the gentle breeze.
Brooks run slowly, locusts hum,
Thus proclaiming, autumn's come.

IF I WERE AN APPLE
Published in *The Instructor, Volume 81*, 1971

If I were an apple
And grew on a tree,
I think I'd drop down
On a nice boy like me.

I wouldn't stay there
Giving nobody joy;
I'd fall down at once
And say, "Eat me, my boy!"

"'To sense each creature singing the hymn of its
existence is to live joyfully in God's love and hope.'
This contemplation of creation allows us to discover in
each thing a teaching which God wishes to hand on
to us, since 'for the believer, to contemplate creation
is to hear a message, to listen to a paradoxical and
silent voice.'" – *Laudato Si'* 85

THE WIND

James J. Metcalfe (1906-1960), published in
Poems for Children, 1950

The wind is warm, the wind is cold,
I never really know,
Until I go outside and see,
The way the wind will blow.

It pushes people on the street,
And rolls their hats away.
It roars in March and whispers in
The merry month of May.

It curls around the chimney and,
It shakes the wooden wall,
And gently guides the autumn leaves
When they begin to fall.

"Now Autumn's fire burns slowly along the woods
And day by day the dead leaves fall and melt."
William Allingham

GOOD-BYE TO SUMMER
Kate S. Kellogg (1854-1925), published in
Child's Calendar Beautiful, 1905

The brown birds are flying
Like leaves through the sky,
The flowerets are calling,
"Dear birdlings, good-by!"

The bird voices falling,
So soft from the sky,
Are answering the flowerets,
"Dear playmates, good-by."

THE SWALLOW
Christina Rossetti (1830-1894), published in
Sing Song, A Nursery Rhyme Book, 1872

Fly away, fly away over the sea,
Sun-loving swallow, for summer is done;
Come again, come again, come back to me,
Bringing the summer and bringing the sun.

"The reason birds can fly and we can't is simply
because they have perfect faith, for to have faith is
to have wings." – J. M. Barrie

COME, LITTLE LEAVES
George Cooper (1838-1927), published in
Mother-song and Child-song, 1896

"Come, little leaves," said the wind one day,
"Come over the meadows with me, and play;
Put on your dresses of red and gold;
Summer is gone, and the days grow cold."

Soon as the leaves heard the wind's loud call,
Down they came fluttering, one and all;
Over the brown fields they danced and flew,
Singing the soft little songs they knew.

"Cricket, good-bye, we've been friends so long;
Little brook, sing us your farewell song.
Say you're sorry to see us go;
Ah! you are sorry, right well we know."

Dancing and whirling the little leaves went;
Winter had called them and they were content.
Soon fast asleep in their earthy beds,
The snow laid a soft mantle over their heads.

"Spring-silver, autumn-gold"
Edna St. Vincent Millay, "Renascence"

THE BIRDS' CONVENTION
Aristophanes (c. 448-c.386 B.C.)

All the birds have come together!
All the birds that I could mention,
Meet to hold a big convention!

How they cluster, how they muster,
How they flitter, flutter, fluster!
Now they dart with gleaming feather,
Now they cuddle all together!

SING
Published in
Our Little Tot's Speaker, 1899

Sing a song of autumn leaves,
Floating lightly down.
Sing of all their changing tints,
From crimson gay to brown;
Sing of asters tall and fair,
Sing of goldenrod,
Sing of elfin acorn-cups,
A-strewing all the sod.

". . . we are called to recognize that other living
beings have a value of their own in God's eyes: 'by
their mere existence they bless him and give him
glory', and indeed, 'the Lord rejoices in all his works'
(Psalms 104:31)." – *Laudato Si'* 69

September 21

STUDY TREES
Published in
Our Little Tot's Speaker, 1899

If everyone I know today
Would study in a hearty way
The trees that all about us stand
To bless and beautify the land,
This world would be a happier sphere
Before there dawned another year.

For lessons sweet and deep and true
Are waiting to be brought to view—
In bough and leaf and root they lurk,
They'd help our play, they'd help our work.
We'd be less selfish, be more kind
If what trees taught us, we should mind.

Then wouldn't you study them with care
To find the secrets rich and rare?
Then won't you open both your eyes
And learn how much trees can surprise?
And when their lovely traits you see
Won't you let trees your pattern be?

"Nature's beauty is mystery and there is nothing to do
but remain open to the surprise."
Wayne Simsic, *Natural Prayer*

TREES

Bliss Carmen (1861-1929), published in
April Airs: A Book of New England Lyrics, 1916

In the Garden of Eden, planted by God,
There were goodly trees in the springing sod,—
Trees of beauty and height and grace,
To stand in splendor before His face.

Apple and hickory, ash and pear,
Oak and beech and the tulip rare,
The trembling aspen, the noble pine,
The sweeping elm by the river line;

Trees for the birds to build and sing,
And the lilac tree for a joy in spring;
Trees to turn at the frosty call
And carpet the ground for their Lord's
footfall;

Trees for fruitage and fire and shade,
Trees for the cunning builder's trade;
Wood for the bow, the spear, and the flail*,
The keel and the mast of the daring sail;

He made them of every grain and girth
For the use of man in the Garden of Earth.
Then lest the soul should not lift her eyes
From the gift to the Giver of Paradise,

On the crown of a hill, for all to see,
God planted a scarlet maple tree.

*Wooden threshing tool

"Everything drew me to love and thank God: people,
trees, plants, and animals. I saw them all as my
kinsfolk; I found on all of them the magic of the name
of Jesus." – *The Way of the Pilgrim*

THE LEAFLETS
Kate Louise Brown (1837- 1921), published in
The Plant Baby and Its Friends, 1897

Fall, little leaflets, fall!
Your mission is not sped;
Shrill pipes the winter wind,
And the happy summer's dead.
Make now a blanket warm
For the flowers, till spring winds call;
You must carpet the waiting earth,
So, fall, little leaflets, fall!

ROBIN REDBREAST: A CHILD'S SONG
William Allingham (1824-1889), published in
Songs, Ballads, and Stories, 1877

Good-bye, good-bye to Summer!
For Summer's nearly done;
The garden smiling faintly,
Cool breezes in the sun;
Our Thrushes now are silent,
Our Swallows flown away—
But Robin's here, in coat of brown,
With ruddy breast-knot gay.
Robin, Robin Redbreast,
    O Robin dear!
Robin singing sweetly
In the falling of the year.

"In the Judeo-Christian tradition, the word 'creation' has a broader meaning than 'nature,' for it has to do with God's loving plan in which every creature has its own value and significance." – *Laudato Si'* 76

A CHILD'S FANCIES IN AUTUMN
Published in *School Education,*
Volume 18: Issue 7, 1899

The maple is a dainty maid,
The pet of all the wood,
Who lights the dusky forest glade
With scarlet cloak and hood.

The elm a lovely lady is,
In shimmering robes of gold,
That catch the sunlight when she moves,
And glisten, fold on fold.

The sumac is a gypsy queen,
Who flaunts in crimson dressed,
And wild along the roadside runs,
Red blossoms in her breast.

And towering high above the wood,
All in his purple cloak,
A monarch in his splendor is
The proud and princely oak.

Children, thank God for these great trees,
That fan the land with every breeze,
Whose drooping branches form cool bowers—
    For these, thank God.

"It is not so much for its beauty that the forest makes a claim upon men's hearts, as for the subtle something, that quality of air, that emanation from old trees, that so wonderfully changes and renews a weary spirit."
Robert Lewis Stevenson

September 25

LOST: THE SUMMER

R. M. Alden, published in *Nature in Verse, A Poetry Reader for Children*, 1895

Where has the summer gone?
She was here just a minute ago,
　　With roses and daisies
　　To whisper her praises—
And everyone loved her so!

Has anyone seen her about?
　She must have gone off in the night!
　　And she took the best flowers
　　And the happiest hours,
　And asked no one's leave for her flight.

Have you noticed her steps in the grass?
　The garden looks red where she went;
　　By the side of the hedge
　　There's a goldenrod edge,
　And the rose-vines are withered and bent.

Don't you fear she is sorry she went?
　It seems but a minute since May!
　　I'm scarcely half through
　　What I wanted to do;
　If she only had waited a day!

Do you think she will ever come back?
　I shall watch every day at the gate
　　For the robins and clover,
　　Saying over and over:
"I know she will come, if I wait!"

"Ecology studies the relationship between living organisms and the environment in which they develop. . . . It cannot be emphasized enough how everything is interconnected. Time and space are not independent of one another . . ." – *Laudato Si'* 138

APPLE-TREE INN

Nancy Byrd Turner (1880-1971), published in
In Playland, 1911

It stands by the roadside, cool-shuttered and high,
  With cordial welcome for all who pass by;
And here's how you enter—you make a quick dash
And scale the steep stair with a bound, in a flash.
You cross the clean threshold and find you a chair.
There's room for all comers and plenty to spare.
You can rock, you can rest, happy lodging you win
  Who stop for an hour at Apple-tree Inn.

The walls and the roof and the ceiling are green,
With rifts of light blue that are painted between.
The seats are upholstered in brown and dark gray,
  And yet, for it all, not a penny to pay.
Then, when you are hungry, the table is spread
With fare that is dainty, delicious, and red.
Oh, hurry and come if you never have been
A guest in your travels at Apple-tree Inn!

"The trees are roofs:
Hollow caverns of cool blue shadow,
Solemn arches
In the afternoons." – John Gould Fletcher

ST. VINCENT DE PAUL

Robert Hugh Benson (1871-1914), published in
An Alphabet of Saints, 1906

"V" is a Frenchman, ST. VINCENT of
PAUL,
Who served as a slave to the Turks first of all;
No Saint is impatient, wherever he be,
But probably VINCENT prayed hard to be
free,
Till GOD had compassion on him in his pain
And brought him back safe to his country again.
There he founded an Order of Sisters; perhaps
You have seen them in London, with large
flapping caps?
They look after the poor and the sick, all
for love,
While St. VINCENT prays for them in
Heaven above.

(ST. VINCENT OF PAUL, Confessor, Founder of the
Congregation of the Mission, and of the Sisters of
Charity; Born at Puy, in Gascony, France, April 24,
1576; Died in Paris, September 27, 1660. Feast,
September 27)

"Cure the sick, raise the dead, cleanse lepers, drive
out demons. Without cost you have received; without
cost you are to give." – Matthew 10:8

September 28

THE RIPENED LEAVES

Margaret Sangster (1838-1912), published in *Little Knights and Ladies: Verses for Young People*, 1895

S aid the leaves upon the branches
One sunny autumn day:
"We've finished all our work, and now
We can no longer stay.
So our gowns of red and yellow,
And our cloaks of sober brown,
Must be worn before the frost comes
And we go rustling down.

"We've had a jolly summer,
With the birds that built their nests
Beneath our green umbrellas,
And the squirrels that were our quests.
But we cannot wait for winter,
And we do not care for snow;
When we hear the wild northwesters
We loose our clasp and go.

"But we hold our heads up bravely
Unto the very last,
And shine in pomp and splendor
As away we flutter fast.
In the mellow autumn noontide
We kiss and say good-by,
And through the naked branches
Then may children see the sky.

". . . each creature has its own purpose. None is superfluous. The entire material universe speaks of God's love, his boundless affection for us. Soil, water, mountains: everything is, as it were, a caress of God."
Laudato Si' 84

September 29
Saints Michael, Gabriel, and Raphael, Archangels

"M" IS FOR SAINT MICHAEL

Hilda van Stockum (1908-2006), published in
Angels' Alphabet, 1948

Whenever I fear
That the Devil is near,
Perhaps right under my bed,
I close my eyes tight
And with all my might
I think of Saint Michael instead.

Of the angels' choir
There's no one higher
He is the captain of all
And he'll be right there
With flaming hair
The minute I softly call.

The Devil he quakes
In his shoes he shakes
When he thinks of Saint Michael's sword.
For no gallant knight
Is so shining bright
As this champion of the Lord.

"Be sober and vigilant. Your opponent the devil is
prowling around like a roaring lion looking for
[someone] to devour." – 1 Peter 5:8

St. Jerome
Robert Hugh Benson (1871-1914), published in
An Alphabet of Saints, 1906

"J" for ST. JEROME, a learned old Priest,
Who left his own country to live in the East.
One day as he walked in the desert he saw
A lion that limped with a thorn in its paw;
So he pulled out the thorn, and the lion,
    content
With his doctor and friend, went wherever he
    went.
The birds loved him too; with the lion and them
He lived in the stable at sweet Bethlehem,
    And there where our LORD and His
        Mother once trod
    He translated the Bible that tells us of GOD.

(ST. JEROME, Priest, Confessor, and Doctor of the
Church; Born in Dalmatia, 346; Died at Bethlehem, 420.
Feast, September 30)

"There are also many other things that Jesus did, but if
these were to be described individually, I do not think
the whole world would contain the books that would
be written." – John 21:25

OCTOBER

GOD'S WORLD

Edna St. Vincent Millay (1892-1950), published in
Renascence and Other Poems, 1917

O world, I cannot hold thee close enough!
Thy winds, thy wide grey skies!
Thy mists that roll and rise!
Thy woods, this autumn day, that ache and sag
And all but cry with color! That gaunt crag
To crush! To lift the lean of that black bluff!
World, World, I cannot get thee close enough!
Long have I known a glory in it all,
But never knew I this;
Here such a passion is
As stretcheth me apart. Lord, I do fear
Thou'st made the world too beautiful this year.
My soul is all but out of me, let fall
No burning leaf; prithee, let no bird call.

"Then I heard every creature in heaven and on earth and under the earth and in the sea, everything in the universe, cry out: 'To the one who sits on the throne and to the Lamb be blessing and honor, glory and might, forever and ever.'" – Revelation 5:13

October 1
St. Therese of the Child Jesus

THE LITTLE FLOWER

Sister Mary Josita Belger (1899-1978), published in
Sing a Song of Holy Things, 1945

F lower of the mountain!
Little Therese!
Sweet child of Jesus' own Heart!

Show us your little way.
Help us all to obey.
Teach us your heavenly art.

You who were dear to Him,
Keep us all near to Him.
Look down, dear saint, from above.

Help us to live like you
In all we say and do.
Dear little child of God's love.

"Just as the sun shines simultaneously on the tall cedars and on each little flower as though it were alone on the earth, so Our Lord is occupied particularly with each soul as though there were no others like it." – St. Therese

GUARDIAN ANGELS
Published in
The Book of the Holy Child, 1947

Oh! My good angel,
Kind and dear!
How glad I am
That you are here.
Stay close by me
All day and night;
And help me do
All that is right.

Beautiful Angel!
My Guardian so mild,
Tenderly guide me,
For I am thy child.

"For he commands his angels with regard to you, to guard you wherever you go." – Psalms 91:11

BURDOCK

Kate Louise Brown (1837- 1921), published in
The Plant Baby and Its Friends, 1897

"Good for play!" said a child, perplext
To know what frolic was coming next;
So she gathered the burrs that all despised,
And her city playmates were quite surprised
To see what a beautiful basket or chair
Could be made, with a little time and care.
They ranged their treasures about with pride,
And played all day by the burdock's side.

Nothing is lost in this world of ours;
Honey comes from the idle flowers;
The weed which we pass in utter scorn
May save a life by another morn.
Wonders await us at every turn;
We must be silent and gladly learn.
No room for recklessness or abuse,
Since even a burdock has its use.

"While we are born with curiosity and wonder and our
early years full of the adventure they bring, I know
such inherent joys are often lost. I also know that,
being deep within us, their latent glow can be fanned
to flame again by awareness and an open mind."
Sigurd F. Olson

October 4
St. Francis

SAINT FRANCIS

Sister Mary Josita Belger (1899-1978), published in
Sing a Song of Holy Things, 1945

Francis loved the birds, the bees,
And all God's wonder-land.
He called the beasts his brothers,
And fed them from his hand.
He sang a song to Sister Moon,
And one to Brother Sun,
For all were God's fair creatures,
And to him a load of fun.

He liked to see the pretty flowers
Come out in early spring,
And all the tall green shade trees
Would cause his heart to sing.
But best of all he loved his God
He loved his Savior most,
His God upon the altar,
His God within the Host.

"Just as happens when we fall in love with someone, whenever he [St. Francis] would gaze at the sun, the moon or the smallest of animals, he burst into song, drawing all other creatures into his praise. He communed with all creation, even preaching to the flowers, inviting them 'to praise the Lord, just as if they were endowed with reason.' . . . If we approach nature and the environment without this openness to awe and wonder, if we no longer speak the language of fraternity and beauty in our relationship with the world, our attitude will be that of masters, consumers, ruthless exploiters . . ." – *Laudato Si'* 11

A BUSY DAY
Lucy Diamond, published in
Our Wonder World, 1914

Mr. Squirrel is so busy

On this bright October day;
Soon the winter will be coming,
So he has no time for play.
Nuts all crisp and brown he gathers;
"I must put them by," says he,
"Where no little boy can find them,
In my pantry in the tree."

"Imagine . . . what it would be like to try to survive
where you actually live, entirely from within your
ecosystem, so that you provide all the necessities of
water, food, clothing, and shelter from the immediate
surrounding area of, say, three or four acres."
Benjamin Wiker, *In Defense of Nature*

GENTIAN

Kate Louise Brown (1837-1921), published in
The Plant Baby and Its Friends, 1897

In spring I found the violet
And rosy mayflower sweet;
And next white-fingered daisy
Was courtesying at my feet.

Then wild rose swung her censer,
And, in a secret hour,
The lonely meadow flamed abroad
With gorgeous cardinal flower.

Some golden-rod close followed,
And aster's gentle eye;
Now withered leaves and dying sod
Beneath a somber sky.

I start! Among the grasses
What eyes of heaven-blue gleam,
All darkly fringed with lashes,
Beside the quiet stream!

Oh, glance of true affection!
The gentian still is here;
The promise set 'mid fading,
The darling of the year.

"Living our vocation to be protectors of God's
handiwork is essential to a life of virtue; it is not an
optional or a secondary aspect of our Christian
experience." – *Laudato Si'* 217

OUR LADY'S ROSARY

Sister Mary Josita Belger (1899-1978), published in
Sing a Song of Holy Things, 1945

I like my little rosary beads

With chains all in between.
Some rosaries are black or white,
Some red, or blue, or green.

The rosary is a flower crown
For our Blessed Lady's hair.
I know she likes the pretty flowers
That make this holy prayer.

She sits upon her starry throne
With Jesus on her knee.
I kneel and say "Hail Mary,"
And she listens lovingly.

I think our Lady smiles sometimes,
And Baby Jesus, too.
He likes to see the pretty wreath,
As all wee children do.

I think He claps His tiny hands
When all my prayer is through,
And laughs a gentle little laugh,
And smells the flowers, too.

Then I say: "Sweet Lady, take
This crown of rose-buds red."
And lovingly I place it
Upon our Lady's head.

"We need to learn to listen." – Pope Francis

FLOWER LULLABY

Addie Litchfield, published in
Child's Calendar Beautiful, 1905

All of the flowers are going to bed,
Daisies are nodding their pretty white heads,
Clovers have softly just whispered "Good night,"
Soon Mother Nature will tuck them up tight.
"Lullaby, lullaby," now the winds sigh,
"Mother will watch you while winter is nigh;"
Over them softly she spreads a white sheet,
"Lullaby, lullaby, sleep, babies, sleep."
Softly, so softly, she's calling them all;
"Hasten, oh, bluebells, or night shades will fall;
Buttercups, buttercups, come to your rest,
Little forget-me-not is all undressed.
Maples are taking off dresses of green.
And in bright dressing-gowns now can be seen;
Oak trees are going more slowly to bed,
With pretty night-caps of dark brown and red."

"Nature gives to every time and season, some
beauties of its own." – Charles Dickens

OCTOBER'S PARTY
George Cooper (1840-1927), included in "School Record:
Volume 6, Issue 2," 1897

O ctober gave a party;
The leaves by hundreds came—
The Chestnuts, Oaks, and Maples,
And leaves of every name.
The Sunshine spread a carpet,
And everything was grand,
Miss Weather led the dancing,
Professor Wind the band.

The Chestnuts came in yellow,
The Oaks in crimson dressed;
The lovely Misses Maple
In scarlet looked their best;
All balanced to their partners,
And gaily fluttered by;
The sight was like a rainbow
New fallen from the sky.

Then, in the rustic hollow,
At hide-and-seek they played,
The party closed at sundown,
And everybody stayed.
Professor Wind played louder;
They flew along the ground;
And then the party ended
In jolly "hands around."

"Man is not alone in celebrating God. To praise Him is
to join all things in their song to Him. Our kinship with
nature is a kinship of praise." – Abraham Heschel

INDIAN SUMMER
W. Wilfred Campbell (1858-1918), published in
The Poems of Wilfred Campbell, 1905

A long the line of smoky hills
The crimson forest stands,
And all the day the blue-jay calls
Throughout the autumn lands.

Now by the brook the maple leans
With all his glory spread,
And all the sumacs on the hills
Have turned their green to red.

Now by great marshes wrapped in mist,
Or past some river's mouth,
Throughout the long, still autumn day
Wild birds are flying south.

"In October, a maple tree before your window lights
up your room like a great lamp. Even on cloudy days,
its presence helps to dispel the gloom."
John Burroughs

THE TOAD'S GOOD-BYE TO THE CHILDREN

Charlotte Mary Yonge (1823-1901), published in
Aunt Charlotte's Evenings at Home with the Poets, 1881

Good-bye, little children, I'm going away,
In my snug little home all winter to stay.
I seldom get up, once I'm tucked in my bed,
And as it grows colder I cover my head.

I sleep very quietly all winter through,
And really enjoy it; there's nothing to do,
The flies are all gone, so there's nothing to eat,
And I take this time to enjoy a good sleep.

My bed is a nice little hole in the ground,
Where snug as a bug in the winter I'm found.
You might think long fasting would make me
    grow thin,
But no! I stay plump as when I go in.

And now, little children, good-bye, one and all,
Some warm day next spring I shall give you a
    call;
I'm quite sure to know when to get out of bed,—
When I feel the warm sun shining down on my
    head.

"We can never have enough of nature."
Henry David Thoreau

October 12

LITTLE HICKORY NUT
Published in *School and Home:*
Volume 16, 1898

A little brown baby, round and wee,
With kind winds to rock him, slept under a tree;
And he grew and he grew, till—I'm sorry to say!
He fell right out of his cradle one day.

Down, down from the treetop, a very bad fall!
But this queer little fellow was not hurt at all;
Now sound and sweet he lies down in the grass,
And there you will find him whenever you pass.

THE LITTLE BIRD UPON THE TREE
Annette Wynne (died 1953), published in
For Days and Days, 1919

The little bird upon the tree
Knows more, far more, than you or me;
And no wise man could teach him how
To hang a nest safe from the bough,
And no wise man need tell him when
It's time to start down south again.

"'To sense each creature singing the hymn of its
existence is to live joyfully in God's love and hope.'"
Christopher J. Thompson, quoting the bishops of
Japan in *The Joyful Mystery*

BEFORE IT'S TIME TO GO TO BED
Annette Wynne (died 1953), published in
For Days and Days, 1919

B efore it's time to go to bed,

Let's have a feast," October said,
"Let's call our family all together.
And celebrate this pleasant weather;"
Then every leaf put on her best,
And each small shrub most richly dressed,
In red and gold and orange, too,
And many another party hue.
The party lasted day and night.
Until the leaves were tired quite,
"Oh, Mother Dear," at last each said,
"It's time for us to go to bed;
Dear Mother Tree, goodnight to you!"
Then loosed her hand and off it flew.
And every little sleepy head
Soon settled in the garden bed,
And dreamed the dreams that flowers do
And slept and slept the winter through.

"The more I study nature, the more I stand amazed at
the work of the Creator." – Robert Boyle

THE GOOD LITTLE LEAVES
Kate Louise Brown (1837- 1921), published in
The Plant Baby and Its Friends, 1897

O ctober came; each leaf was dressed
In red and amber quite its best.
The hills were wrapped in faint blue haze,
And asters smiled in forest ways.

Jack Frost stole out in quiet hours,
He breathed upon the shivering flowers;
They rubbed their eyes, and bowed full low;
They nodded fast—'twas time to go.

The leaves grew sleepy; the great tree said,
"Good night, my children, 'tis time for bed."
So the little leaves did as they were told,
And soon were dreaming in nightgowns of gold.

"And into the forest I go, to lose myself
and find my soul." – Mariah Danu

AUTUMN LEAVES
Angelina Wray, published in
Child's Calendar Beautiful, 1905

In the hush and the lonely silence
Of the chill October night,
Some wizard has worked his magic
With fairy fingers light.
The leaves of the sturdy oak trees
Are splendid with crimson and red,
And the golden flags of the maple
Are fluttering overhead.

Through the tangle of faded grasses
There are trailing vines ablaze,
And the glory of warmth and color
Gleams through the autumn haze,
Like banners of marching armies
That farther and farther go;
Down the winding roads and valleys
The boughs of the sumacs glow.

So open your eyes, little children,
And open your hearts as well,
Till the charm of the bright October
Shall fold you in its spell.

"How beautiful the leaves grow old. How full of light
and color are their last days." – John Burroughs

October 16

THE LEAVES
Published in *The Book of 1,000 Poems*, 1998

The leaves had a wonderful frolic.
They danced to the wind's loud song.
They whirled, and they floated, and scampered.
They circled and flew along.

The moon saw the little leaves dancing.
Each looked like a small brown bird.
The man in the moon smiled and listened.
And this is the song he heard.

The North Wind is calling, is calling,
And we must whirl round and round,
And then, when our dancing is ended,
We'll make a warm quilt for the ground.

"Climb the mountains and get their good tidings.
Nature's peace will flow into you as sunshine flows
into trees. The winds will blow their own freshness into
you, and the storms their energy, while cares will drop
off like autumn leaves." – John Muir

In Coventry
Rev. James J. Daly (1921-2013), published in
The Bookman, 1922

My friends, the leaves, who used to entertain me
   On summer afternoons with idle chatter,
Are dropping off in ways that shock and pain me.
   I wonder what's the matter.

My friends, the birds, are quietly withdrawing;
   The meadow larks are gone from fence and
      stubble;
Even the crows are gone; I liked their cawing.
   I wonder what's the trouble.

My friend, the sun, is here, but altered slightly;
   He acts more coolly than he has been doing;
He seems more distant, and he smiles less
   brightly.
   I wonder what is brewing.

"Each one of us is called to develop an integral
ecology, an integral spirituality, one that seeks to take
seriously our place on this earth and the vocation to
be His stewards." – Christopher J. Thompson,
The Joyful Mystery

0

WHEN MARY GOES WALKING
Patrick R. Chalmers (1872-1942), published in
Green Days and Blue Days, 1914

When Mary goes walking
The autumn winds blow,
The poplars they curtsey,
The larches bend low;
The oaks and the beeches
Their gold they fling down,
To make her a carpet,
To make her a crown.

"If the simple fact of being human moves people to care for the environment of which they are a part, Christians in their turn 'realize that their responsibility within creation, and their duty towards nature and the Creator, are an essential part of their faith.' It is good for humanity and the world at large when we believers better recognize the ecological commitments which stem from our convictions."
Laudato Si' 64

THE WIND IS A CAT

Edith Romig Fuller (1883-1965), published in
White Peaks and Green, 1928

Wind is a cat
That prowls at night,
Now in a valley,
Now on a height,

Pouncing on houses
Till folks in their beds
Draw all the covers
Over their heads.

It sings to the moon,
It scratches at doors;
It lashes its tail
Around chimneys and roars.
It claws at the clouds
Till it fringes their silk;
It laps up the dawn
Like a saucer of milk;

Then, chasing the stars
To the tops of the firs,
Curls down for a nap
And purrs and purrs.

"For in him were created all things in heaven and on earth, the visible and the invisible, whether thrones or dominions or principalities or powers; all things were created through him and for him." – Colossians 1:16

GOD IS LIKE THIS
Rowena Bennett (1896-1981), published in
The Day Is Dancing, 1948

I cannot see the wind at all
Or hold it in my hand;
And yet I know there is a wind
Because it swirls the sand.
I know there is a wondrous wind,
Because I glimpse its power
Whenever it bends low a tree
Or sways the smallest flower.

And God is very much like this,
Invisible as air;
I cannot touch or see Him, yet
I know that He is there
Because I glimpse His wondrous works
And goodness everywhere.

"The universe unfolds in God, who fills it completely.
Hence, there is a mystical meaning to be found in a
leaf, in a mountain trail, in a dewdrop, in a poor
person's face. The ideal is not only to pass from the
exterior to the interior to discover the action of God in
the soul, but also to discover God in all things."
Laudato Si' 233

AUTUMN FASHIONS

Edith M. Thomas (1854-1925), published in
Young Folks' Recitations: Number 2, 1888

The Maple owned that she was tired of always wearing
green,
She knew that she had grown, of late, too shabby to be
seen!
The Oak and Beech and Chestnut then deplored their
shabbiness,
And all, except the Hemlock sad, were wild to change
their dress.

"For fashion-plate we'll take the flowers," the rustling
Maple said,
"And like the Tulip I'll be clothed in splendid gold and
red!"
"The cheerful Sunflower suits me best," the lightsome
Beech replied;
"The Marigold my choice shall be," the Chestnut spoke
with pride.

The sturdy Oak took time to think—"I hate such glaring
hues;
The Gillyflower, so dark and rich, I for my model choose."
So every tree in all the grove, except the Hemlock sad,
According to its wish ere long in brilliant dress was clad.

And here they stayed through all the soft and bright
October days;
They wished to be like flowers—indeed, they look like
huge bouquets!

"Autumn is a second spring when every leaf
is a flower." – Albert Camus

LEISURE
William Henry Davies (1871-1940), published in
Songs of Joy and Others, 1911

What is this life if, full of care,
We have no time to stand and stare.

No time to stand beneath the boughs
And stare as long as sheep or cows.

No time to see, when woods we pass,
Where squirrels hide their nuts in grass.

No time to see, in broad daylight,
Streams full of stars, like skies at night.

No time to turn at Beauty's glance,
And watch her feet, how they can dance.

No time to wait till her mouth can
Enrich that smile her eyes began.

A poor life this if, full of care,
We have no time to stand and stare.

"What inspired the authors of Job, Ecclesiastes, and
the Psalms if not a world of mystery, capable at any
time of revealing God?" – Wayne Simsic,
Natural Prayer

LITTLE SONG OF LIFE
Lizette Woodworth Reese (1856-1935), published in
Poems of the English Race, 1921

Glad that I live am I;
That the sky is blue;
Glad for the country lanes,
And the fall of dew.

After the sun the rain,
After the rain the sun;
This is the way of life,
Till the work be done.

All that we need to do,
Be we low or high,
Is to see that we grow
Nearer the sky.

"yet, in bestowing his goodness, he did not leave
himself without witness, for he gave you rains from
heaven and fruitful seasons, and filled you with
nourishment and gladness for your hearts."
Acts 14:17

WISE OLD OWL
Traditional Nursery Rhyme

There was an owl lived in an oak
The more he heard, the less he spoke.
The less he spoke, the more he heard.
O, if men were all like that wise bird.

JACK FROST'S MONTH
[FROM "A RHYME OF THE YEAR"]
Published in *Our Little Tot's Speaker*, 1899

October, where's your friend, Jack Frost?
You always come together,
With lovely leaves
On all the trees,
And hazy, dreamy weather.

"Ignorance of the natural world seems to be the new normal." – Christopher J. Thompson, *The Joyful Mystery*

MILKWEED POD

Anna M. Pratt, published in *The American Primary Teacher: Volume 25*, 1901

"Ha! Ha! Don't mind my laughing,
　Excuse a milkweed pod.
I really want to split my sides,
　I feel so very odd.
I am so brimful of nonsense
　I must let my fancies fly."
Out burst the little seeds within:
　"We beg of you to try."

"Ho! Hum! Excuse my yawning.
　I'm a very empty pod.
I think I'm rather sleepy too.
　I'd better take a nod."
"Don't mention it," replied the seeds,
　"'Tis the proper thing to do."
And they floated off—but where they went
　I never heard: Did you?

"There is a nobility in the duty to care for creation
through little daily actions . . . such as avoiding the
use of plastic and paper, reducing water
consumption, separating refuse, cooking only what
can reasonably be consumed, showing care for other
living beings, using public transport or car-pooling,
planting trees, turning off unnecessary lights, or any
number of other practices. . . . Reusing something
instead of immediately discarding it, when done for
the right reasons, can be an act of love which
expresses our own dignity." – *Laudato Si'* 211

THE CHILDREN OF THE STINGING THISTLE
Published in *Little Folks' Speaker*, 1901

I'm but a little thistle
By dusty roads, perchance;
I guard my purple blossoms
With sharp and stinging lance.

But when the summer's over,
And winter draweth near,
I give the winds my children
Without a care or fear.

Away, away, then sailing,
Through hazy skies they fly,
Now, just above the grasses,
Then o'er the treetops, high.

Until within some hollow,
To rest they sink, at last,
And there, all safely sheltered,
They sleep till winter's past.

"When I am dead, I wish my friends to remember that
I always plucked a thistle and planted a rose."
Abraham Lincoln

WILD GEESE

Elinor Chipp (1888-1968), published in
"Telling Tails" magazine, November 1920

I heard the wild geese flying
In the dead of the night,
With the beat of wings and crying
I heard the wild geese flying.

And dreams in my heart sighing
Followed their northward flight.
I heard the wild geese flying
In the dead of the night.

"We understand better the importance and meaning of each creature if we contemplate it within the entirety of God's plan." – *Laudato Si'* 86

THE MOON
Robert Louis Stevenson (1850-1894), published in
A Child's Garden of Verses, 1885

The moon has a face like the clock in the hall;
She shines on thieves on the garden wall,
On streets and fields and harbor quays*,
And birdies asleep in the forks of the trees.

The squalling cat and the squeaking mouse,
The howling dog by the door of the house,
The bat that lies in bed at noon,
All love to be out by the light of the moon.

But all of the things that belong to the day
Cuddle to sleep to be out of her way;
And flowers and children close their eyes
Till up in the morning the sun shall arise.

* docks; piers; landings

". . . everything is intimately present to everything else
in the universe. Nothing is completely itself without
everything else." – Thomas Berry,
The Dream of the Earth

THE KIND MOON
Sara Teasdale (1884-1933), published in
Helen of Troy And Other Poems, 1911

I think the moon is very kind

To take such trouble just for me.
He came along with me from home
    To keep me company.

He went as fast as I could run;
I wonder how he crossed the sky?
I'm sure he hasn't legs and feet
    Or any wings to fly.

Yet here he is above their roof;
Perhaps he thinks it isn't right
For me to go so far alone,
    Though mother said I might.

"The moon like a flower
In heaven's high bower
With silent delight
Sits and smiles on the night."
William Blake, "Songs of Innocence"

THE FOUR WINDS

Frank Dempster Sherman (1860-1916), published in
Nature in Verse, 1895

In winter, when the wind I hear,
I know the clouds will disappear;
For 'tis the wind who sweeps the sky
And piles the snow in ridges high.

In spring, when stirs the wind, I know
That soon the crocus buds will show;
For 'tis the wind who bids them wake
And into pretty blossoms break.

In summer, when it softly blows,
Soon red, I know, will be the rose;
For 'tis the wind to her who speaks,
And brings the blushes to her cheeks.

In autumn, when the wind is up,
I know the acorn's out its cup;
For 'tis the wind who takes it out,
And plants an oak somewhere about.

". . . each creature reflects something of God and
has a message to convey to us. . . . Then too, there is
the recognition that God created the world, writing
into it an order and a dynamism that human beings
have no right to ignore." – *Laudato Si'* 221

October 31

JACK-O'-LANTERN
German Folk Song

Jack-o'-lantern, Jack-o'-lantern
You are such a funny sight
As you sit there in the window
Looking out at the night.
You were once a yellow pumpkin
Growing on a sturdy vine,
Now you are a Jack-o'-lantern
See the candle light shine.

THE CAT OF CATS
William Brighty Rands (1823-1882)

I am the cat of cats. I am
The everlasting cat!
Cunning, and old, and sleek as jam,
The everlasting cat!
I hunt vermin in the night—
The everlasting cat!
For I see best without the light—
The everlasting cat!

"I would rather sit on a pumpkin and have it all to myself than be crowded on a velvet cushion."
Henry David Thoreau

NOVEMBER

EARTH'S LITANY

Sister Maryanna, O.P., published in
A Lovely Gate Set Wide, 1946

I passed a laughing brook today
And as it wound its woodland way,
I thought I heard its waters say:
   "We thank Thee, Lord!"

The fallen leaves, pine needles sweet,
A green-gold carpet 'neath my feet,
Stirred by each passing breeze repeat:
   "We thank Thee, Lord!"

I heard the snowbird's vesper prayer
Fall softly on the evening air
In liquid notes of beauty rare:
   "We thank Thee, Lord!"

Across the sky, star after star
Sends out its jeweled gleams afar —
The words they seem to twinkle are:
   "We thank Thee, Lord!"

Each sharp-eyed, bright-eyed, furry thing,
All forest folk, afoot, awing
In woodland language mutely sing:
   "We thank Thee, Lord!"

Much more should children every day
In time of prayer, or work, or play,
For all God's gifts, and blessings say:
   "We thank Thee, Lord!"

" . .. MAN HAS SPECIFIC RESPONSIBILITY
TOWARDS THE ENVIRONMENT IN WHICH HE
LIVES, TOWARDS THE CREATION WHICH GOD
HAS PUT AT THE SERVICE OF HIS PERSONAL
DIGNITY, OF HIS LIFE, NOT ONLY FOR THE
PRESENT BUT ALSO FOR FUTURE
GENERATIONS." – ST. POPE JOHN PAUL II

FEAST OF ALL SAINTS

Sister Mary Josita Belger (1899-1978), published in
Sing a Song of Holy Things, 1945

There are many saints in heaven,
Saint for every day—
Baby saints and children saints,
And saints quite old and gray.

There are the Holy Innocents
Who died for Jesus' sake,
And little Agnes, holy lamb,
Who did in heaven wake.

And many other children,
Who loved with all their heart,
And gladly giving up their lives
Took heaven for their part.

And holy men and women
Who tried from day to day,
To listen to the voice of God,
And his commands obey.

Today they have a feast-day,
These saints both young and old,
With Mary Queen and Christ our King
On thrones of shining gold.

"And the one who searches hearts knows what is the
intention of the Spirit, because it intercedes for the
holy ones according to God's will." – Romans 8:27

November 2
All Souls

ALL SOULS DAY
Sister Mary Josita Belger (1899-1978), published in
Sing a Song of Holy Things, 1945

Have pity, Lord, on those poor souls
In Purgatory's burning coals.
Let them rest in peace!

They cannot help themselves at all,
But for Your pity always call.
Let them rest in peace!

They love You, Lord, with tender love,
And long to be with You above.
Let them rest in peace!

NOVEMBER NIGHT
Adelaide Crapsey (1878-1914), published in *Verse*, 1922

Listen . . .
With faint dry sound,
Like steps of passing ghosts,
The leaves, frost-crisp'd, break from the trees
And fall.

"So, since the Universe began
And till it shall be ended,
The soul of Nature, the soul of Man
And the soul of God are blended."
"The Mystery of Nature" by Theodore Tilton

THE CAT-TAILS
Published in *Primary Education:*
Volume 2, 1894

F riendly, little cat-tails,
Growing close together,
Crowding marsh and shallow stream
Through all the autumn weather.

Strange, mysterious cat-tails
Children's great delight,
Brown and velvety without,
Within all fluffy white.

"Nature excels in the least things." – Henry David
Thoreau, attributed to Pliny, ancient Roman naturalist

NOVEMBER

Fannie Sewell Whittaker (1869-1961), published in
Songs of the Tree-top and Meadow, 1899

T rees, bare and brown,
Dry leaves everywhere,
Dancing up and down,
Whirling through the air.

Red-cheeked apples roasted,
Popcorn almost done,
Toes and chestnuts toasted,
That's November fun.

NOVEMBER

Published in *How to Celebrate Thanksgiving and
Christmas*, 1894

M y sisters are September and October bright and
gay,
They're beautiful in richer charms, while I am
brown and gray;
Yet all their glorious days cannot compare with one
I bring,
This one—the loveliest of the fall, Thanksgiving
Day, I sing.

"Why are there trees I never walk under but large and
melodious thoughts descend upon me?" – Walt
Whitman, "Song of the Open Road"

THE EMPTY NEST

Alice E. Allen, published in
Child's Calendar Beautiful, 1905

Fly away little bird! Southern skies are aglow,
And our winter is coming in silence and snow;
Take the songs that you taught me on summer
    days fleet,
Take the music you brought, so tender, so sweet.
But leave me this wee nest, so lonely and gray!
    Fly away! Fly away! Fly away!

Fly away little bird, with the bonny red breast!
I remember one day well—we love it the best,—
I found in their cradle, so dreamy and deep,
Blue eggs—bits of music were in them asleep,—
Don't forget this wee nest so empty today!
    Fly away, little bird, fly away!

Fly away, little bird! Through the snow and the
    storm!
I shall know you are singing in groves glad and
    warm;
Next spring, will you bring to me dreams of it all
As sweetly you sing to me from your tree tall?
You'll find your nest waiting that morning in May,
    Fly away! Fly away! Fly away!

"He made from one the whole human race to dwell
on the entire surface of the earth, and he fixed the
ordered seasons and the boundaries of their regions,
so that people might seek God, even perhaps grope
for him and find him, though indeed he is not far from
any one of us." – Acts 17:26-27

NOVEMBER
Alice Cary (1820-1871), published in *The Poetical Works of Alice and Phoebe Cary*, 1884

The leaves are fading and falling,
The winds are rough and wild,
The birds have ceased their calling,
But let me tell you, my child,

Though day by day, as it closes,
Doth darker and colder grow,
The roots of the bright red roses
Will keep alive in the snow.

And when the Winter is over,
The boughs will get new leaves,
The quail come back to the clover,
And the swallow back to the eaves. . . .

The leaves today are whirling,
The brooks are dry and dumb,
But let me tell you, my darling,
The Spring will be sure to come.

There must be rough, cold weather,
And winds and rains so wild;
Not all good things together
Come to us here, my child.

So, when some dear joy loses
Its beauteous summer glow,
Think how the roots of the roses
Are kept alive in the snow.

"To understand the wild you must first understand the woods." – Robert Macfarlane, *The Wild Places*

MOON, SO ROUND AND YELLOW

Matthias Barr (1831-1931), published in
The Child's Garland of Little Poems, 1866

M oon, so round and yellow,

Looking from on high,
How I love to see you
Shining in the sky.
Oft and oft I wonder,
When I see you there,
How they get to light you,
Hanging in the air:

Where you go at morning,
When the night is past,
And the sun comes peeping
O'er the hills at last.
Sometime I will watch you
Slyly overhead,
When you think I'm sleeping
Snugly in my bed.

"To one who has been long in city pent,
'Tis very sweet to look into the fair
And open face of heaven." – John Keats

EACH IN HIS OWN TONGUE (FROM)
William Herbert Carruth (1859-1924), published in
Each in His Own Tongue and Other Poems, 1909

Ahaze on the far horizon,
The infinite, tender sky,
The ripe rich tint of the cornfields,
And the wild geese sailing high—
And all over upland and lowland
The charm of the golden-rod—
Some of us call it Autumn
And others call it God.

"An integral ecology includes taking time to recover a serene harmony with creation, reflecting on our lifestyle and our ideals, and contemplating the Creator who lives among us and surrounds us, whose presence 'must not be contrived but found, uncovered.'" – *Laudato Si* 225

WHAT DO THE STARS DO?

Christina Rossetti (1830-1894), published in
Sing Song, A Nursery Rhyme Book, 1872

What do the stars do
Up in the sky,
Higher than the wind can blow,
Or the clouds can fly?

Each star in its own glory
Circles, circles still;
As it was lit to shine and set,
And do its Maker's will.

THE PLEIADS*

Fr. John B. Tabb (1845-1909), published in
Child Verse, 1899

"Who are you with clustered light,
  Little Sisters seven?"
"Crickets chirping all the night
  On the hearth of heaven."

* a star-cluster visible in the east in November

". . . beneath the black-blue quilt of a starry night the
urge to pray is irrepressible because prayer is the most
intelligent response to the splendor of things."
Christopher J. Thompson, *The Joyful Mystery*

November 10

THE PINEWOOD PEOPLE

Elizabeth Thornton Turner (1884-1962), published in
A Jolly Jingle-Book, 1913

When winds are noisy-winged and high,
   And crystal-clear the day,
Down where the forest meets the sky
   The Pinewood People play.

Far off I see them bow, advance,
   Swing partners and retreat,
As though some slow, old-fashioned dance
   Had claimed their tripping feet.

Or hand to hand they wave, and so,
   With dip and bend and swing,
Through "tag" and "hide" and "touch and go"
   They flutter, frolicking.

But when I run to join the play,
   I find my search is vain.
Always they see me on the way,
   And change to pines again.

"Between every two pines is the doorway to a
new world." – John Muir

ST. MARTIN OF TOURS

Robert Hugh Benson (1871-1914), published in
An Alphabet of Saints, 1906

"M" for SAINT MARTIN, in Mitre and
   Cope
(The Bishop of Tours, not St. MARTIN the Pope);
His father, a soldier, disliked and despised
The True Faith, and prevented his being baptized
By making him serve in the army of Gaul,
Though he wasn't that sort of a soldier at all.
At Amiens one day, in the wind and the sleet,
He was stopped by a beggar who begged in the street;
He'd no money to give, so he made a great tear
In his cloak and gave part to the beggar to wear.

That night in a vision St. MARTIN was shown
Our LORD as He reigns on His heavenly Throne;
He was wearing the piece that the beggar had worn!
For CHRIST takes what we give to the poor and forlorn.

(ST. MARTIN of TOURS, Bishop and Confessor, called
"Apostle of Gaul"; Born in Pannonia, 316; Founded the
first French Monastery near Poiters, 360; Bishop of
Tours, 372; Died 396. Feast, November 11)

"He said to them in reply, 'Whoever has two tunics
should share with the person who has none. And
whoever has food should do likewise.'" – Luke 3:11

NOVEMBER

Ada Shelton, published in *The Journal of Education:*
Volumes 41-42, 1895

O dear, old, dull November,
  They don't speak well of you;
They say your winds are chilling,
  Your skies are seldom blue.
They tell how you go sighing
  Among the leafless trees,
You have no warmth nor brightness,
  All kinds of things like these.

But dearie me, November!
  They quite forget to speak
About the wealth of color
  On each round apple's cheek;
How yellow is each pumpkin
  That in the cornfield lies,
Almost as good as sunshine
  And better still for pies.

O yes, dear, old November,
  You've lots of pleasant things.
All through the month we're longing
  To taste your turkey wings.
What if you're dull a trifle,
  Or just a little gray?
If not for you, we'd never have
  Dear old Thanksgiving Day.

"There are no dreary sights; only dreary sightseers."
C. S. Lewis

FRIENDS
L. G. Warner, published in
Songs of the Tree-top and Meadow, 1899

North wind came whistling through the wood,
  Where the tender, sweet things grew—
The tall fair ferns and the maiden's hair
  And the gentle gentians blue.
"It is very cold! Are we growing old?"
  They sighed, "What shall we do?"

The sigh went up to the loving leaves, —
  "We must help," they whispered low.
"They are frightened and weak, O brave old trees!
  But we love you well, you know."
And the trees said, "We are strong—make haste!
  Down to the darlings go."

So the leaves went floating, floating down,
  All yellow, and brown, and red,
And the frail little trembling, thankful things
  Lay still, and were comforted.
And the blue sky smiled through the bare old trees
  Down on their safe warm bed.

"Enter these enchanted woods,
You who dare." – George Meredith

MRS. RED SQUIRREL
Published in *The Autumn Months*, 1907

Mrs. Red Squirrel sat on the top of a tree;
"I believe in the habit of saving," said she;
"If it were not for that, in the cold winter weather
I should starve, and my young ones, I know,
    altogether;
But I am teaching my children to run and lay up
Every acorn as soon as it drops from its cup,
And to get out the corn from the shocks in the field—
There's a nice hollow tree where I keep it concealed.

"We have laid up some wheat, and some barley and
    rye,
And some very nice pumpkin seeds I have put by;
Best of all, we have gathered in all that we could
Of beechnuts and butternuts grown in the wood;
For cold days and hard times winter surely will bring.
And a habit of saving's an excellent thing.

"But my children—you know how young squirrels like
    play,
'We have plenty, great plenty, already,' they say;
'We are tired of bringing in food for our store;
Let us all have a frolic, and gather no more!'
But I tell them it's pleasant when winter is rough,
If we feel both to use and to give we've enough;
And they'll find, ere the butternuts bloom in the spring,
That a habit of saving's an excellent thing."

"There is presently no other way for humans to
educate themselves for survival and fulfillment than
through the instruction available through the natural
world." – Thomas Berry, *The Dream of the Earth*

AUTUMN (FROM "THE CIRCLING YEAR")
Ramona Graham, published in *Normal Instructor and
Primary Plans: Volume 30*, 1920

A cold, gray day, a lowering sky,

A lonesome pigeon wheeling by;
The soft, blue smoke that hangs and fades,
The shivering crane that flaps and wades;
Dead leaves that, whispering, quit their tree,
The peace the river sings to me;
The chill aloofness of the Fall—
I love it all!

"If someone has not learned to stop and admire
something beautiful, we should not be surprised if he
or she treats everything as an object to be used and
abused without scruple. If we want to bring about
deep change, we need to realize that certain
mindsets really do influence our behavior. Our efforts
at education will be inadequate and ineffectual
unless we strive to promote a new way of thinking
about human beings, life, society and our relationship
with nature." – *Laudato Si'* 215

THE SUNSHINE (FROM)

Mary Howitt (1799-1888), published in *The Poetical Works of Mary Howitt, Eliza Cook and L.E.L.*, 1855

I love the sunshine everywhere—
    In wood and field, and glen;
I love it in the busy haunts
    Of town-imprisoned men. . . .

Oh! Yes; I love the sunshine!
    Like kindness or like mirth,
Upon a human countenance
    Is sunshine on the earth!

Upon the earth; upon the sea;
    And through the crystal air,
On piled up clouds; the gracious sun;
    Is glorious everywhere.

"I realize that I do not live on the earth but in relationship with it." – Wayne Simsic, *Natural Prayer*

November 17
St. Elizabeth of Hungary

Saint Elizabeth
Sister Mary Josita Belger (1899-1978), published in
Sing a Song of Holy Things, 1945

Many, many years ago
There lived a lovely queen.
Her beautiful, great love for God
By Him alone was seen.

Her name was Queen Elizabeth,
This lovely lady fair,
And each day she went walking
In the fresh, cold winter air.
But what was that she carried
Within her basket brown?
It was food for all God's suffering poor
Who lived about the town.

One day she met her husband
As she walked along the road.
He wondered what she carried
That seemed so great a load.

He opened wide her mantle,
And what was his surprise!
Her arms were filled with roses
Before his very eyes.

The king then knew that God had worked
A miracle of grace.
He thanked Him for this holy wife,
And kissed her lovely face.

"Today, however, we have to realize that a true ecological approach *always* becomes a social approach;
it must integrate questions of justice in debates on the
environment, so as to hear *both the cry of the earth
and the cry of the poor*." – *Laudato Si'* 49

THE GREAT BROWN OWL

Jane Euphemia Brown (1811-1898), published in
Easy Poetry for Children, 1865

The brown owl sits in the ivy bush,
And she looks wondrous wise,
With a horny beak beneath her cowl,
And a pair of large round eyes.

She sat all day on the selfsame spray,
From sunrise till sunset;
And the dim, grey light it was all too bright
For the owl to see in yet.

"Jenny Owlet, Jenny Owlet," said a merry
     little bird,
"They say you're wondrous wise;
But I don't think you see, though you're
     looking at me
With your large, round, shining eyes."

But night came soon, and the pale white moon
Rolled high up in the skies;
And the great brown owl flew away in her cowl*,
With her large, round, shining eyes.

* a large, loose hood

"Earth is crammed with heaven, and every common
bush afire with God, but only he who sees takes off his
shoes." – Elizabeth Barrett Browning

JACK FROST

Published in *The Golden Flute: An Anthology of Poetry
for Young Children,* 1932

When Jack Frost comes—oh! the fun.
He plays his pranks on everyone.
He'll pinch your nose and bite your toes,
But where he goes—nobody knows.

He paints upon the window-pane:
Tin soldiers, teddy-bears and trains.
He nips the leaves from off the trees—
This little man—nobody sees.

[Regarding St. Pope John Paul II]: "He always
preserved that sense of wonder, like that of a child
who does not take creation for granted." – Leno Zani,
The Secret Life of John Paul II

IF ALL THE SKIES

Henry van Dyke (1853-1933), published in *The Works of Henry van Dyke: Poems*, 1920

If all the skies were sunshine,
  Our faces would be fain*
To feel once more upon them
  The cooling splash of rain.

If all the world were music,
  Our hearts would often long
For one sweet strain of silence,
  To break the endless song.

If life were always merry,
  Our souls would seek relief,
And rest from weary laughter
  In the quiet arms of grief.

* obliged; pleased; willing

"The royal road to knowledge, all may win, who seek the source of life in everything." – Edwin Leibfreed

OUR LADY'S PRESENTATION

Rev. Gerald M.C. Fitzgerald (1894-1969), published in
Paths from Bethlehem, 1937

Who is this little one? He said,
The High Priest bowed his aged head,
To catch the answer of a child.
He heard, and gravely then he smiled.
"I am the Handmaid of the Lord!"

So young, and yet so full of grace,
The matrons watched her upturned face,
Yet dropped their eyes before her gaze,
Where shone God's holiness ablaze—
She was the Handmaid of the Lord.

Anna and holy Joachim
Stood back within the shadows dim,
The mother soothed his breaking heart
"Our child doth choose the better part,
She is the Handmaid of the Lord!"

"Mary said, 'Behold, I am the handmaid of the Lord.
May it be done to me according to your word.' Then
the angel departed from her." – Luke 1:38

DOWN TO SLEEP
Helen Hunt Jackson (1830-1885), published in
The Autumn Months, 1907

November woods are bare and still,
November days are clear and bright.
Each noon burns up the morning's chill,
The morning's snow is gone by night.
Each day my steps grow slow, grow light,
As through the woods I reverent creep.
Watching all things "lie down to sleep. . . ."

"Unplanned contemplation comes softly as falling
mist or the first snows of autumn." – Sigurd Olson

THE PILGRIMS CAME
Annette Wynne (died 1953), published in
For Days and Days, 1919

The Pilgrims came across the sea,
　And never thought of you and me;
And yet it's very strange the way
　We think of them Thanksgiving day.

We tell their story, old and true
　Of how they sailed across the blue,
And found a new land to be free
　And built their homes quite near the sea.

Every child knows well the tale
　Of how they bravely turned the sail,
And journeyed many a day and night,
　To worship God as they thought right.

The people think that they were sad
　And grave; I'm sure that they were glad—
They made Thanksgiving Day—that's fun—
　We thank the Pilgrims every one!

"'Let the heaven and the earth praise him,
the seas and whatever moves in them!'"
Psalms 69:35

THANKSGIVING DAY ACROSTIC
N. H., published in *Teacher's World*, 1895

Thanksgiving Day has come once more
Hurrah! For all the autumn store;
Apples, fruits and nuts and grain
Now plentiful and ripe again.
Kind Nature spreads the mighty feast,
Sending her gifts now west, now east;
Gives to us all our harvest time,
In many a land, in many a clime.
Very thankfully here we stand,
In turn we view on every hand,
Not only useful things but gay,
Given for this Thanksgiving Day.

"I would maintain that thanks are the highest form of thought; and that gratitude is happiness doubled by wonder." – G. K. Chesterton

ST. KATHERINE OF ALEXANDRIA

Robert Hugh Benson (1871-1914), published in
An Alphabet of Saints, 1906

"K" for ST. KATHERINE, Martyr, you see;
She was learned and lovely and good as could be;
She knew mathematics, and learnt how to speak
And to read and to write both in Latin and Greek.
She once had a vision that JESUS, her King,
Came and made her His Own with a gold wedding
    ring.
Soon after this vision, King Maximin came
And offered her marriage and riches and fame:
"I'll make you my Empress, if you will deny
The name of CHRIST JESUS—if not, you shall die."
"I will die," she replied; and was tied to a wheel
That was all covered over with razors of steel;
But the lightning destroyed it, so Maximin said,
"Take her out of the city and cut off her head."
    St. KATHERINE'S body by Angels was carried
    To Sinai's summit, where MOSES had tarried;
    A Martyr and Virgin, she wears the gold ring
    She received from CHRIST JESUS, the Heavenly
    King.

(ST. KATHERINE of ALEXANDRIA, Virgin and
Martyr; Born at Alexandria about 280; Martyred, 307.
Feast, November 25)

"Tell the rich in the present age not to be proud and
not to rely on so uncertain a thing as wealth but
rather on God, who richly provides us with all things
for our enjoyment." – 1 Timothy 6:17

THANKSGIVING SONG
D. H., published in *Child-Garden of Story,
Song and Play*, 1894

The happy thank-you day has come,
And harvest time is past,
We've gathered fruits and nuts and grains,
We'll say good-bye at last;
Good-bye to Autumn, Autumn dear,
And with our parting words
We'll sing our thanks to God above,
For fruit and trees and birds.

WE THANK THEE
Margaret B. Songster, published in
Child's Calendar Beautiful, 1905

For peace and for plenty, for freedom, for rest,
For joy in the land from the east to the west,
For the dear starry flag, with its red, white and
blue.
We thank thee from hearts that are honest and
true.
For waking and sleeping, for blessings to be.
We children would offer our praises to thee!
For God is our Father and bends from above
To keep the round world in the smile of His love.

"The United States themselves are essentially the
greatest poem." – Walt Whitman

SUNBEAM

Emilie Poulsson (1853-1939), published in *Rules and Regulations and Course of Study for Use in the Public Schools of Wheaton, Illinois*, 1900

"What shall I send to the earth today?"
    Said the great, round golden sun.
"Let us go down to work and play!"
    Said the sunbeams, every one.

Down to the earth the sunbeams crept,
    To children in their beds,
Touching the eyes of those who slept,
    And gilding the little heads.

"Wake, little children!" they cried in glee,
    "And from dreamland come away!
We've brought you a present! Wake and see!
    We've brought you a sunny day!"

A SUNSET

Mary Carolyn Davies (1888-1940?), published in
A Little Freckled Person, 1919

Life seems so sweet! I don't know why,—
Perhaps 'tis just because the sky
Put on, tonight, to make me glad,
A dress I didn't know she had.

"The sky broke like an egg into full sunset and the water caught fire." – Pamela Hansford Johnson

WE THANK THEE

Unknown although often erroneously attributed to
Ralph Waldo Emerson, published in
Little Workers: Volume 1, 1884

For flowers that bloom about our feet;
For tender grass, so fresh, so sweet;
For song of bird, and hum of bee;
For all things fair we hear or see,
  Father in heaven, we thank Thee.
For blue of stream and blue of sky;
For pleasant shade of branches high;
For fragrant air and cooling breeze;
For beauty of the blooming trees,
  Father in heaven, we thank Thee.
For mother-love and father-care,
For brothers strong and sisters fair,
For love at home and here each day,
For guidance, lest we go astray,
  Father in Heaven, we thank Thee!.
For thy everlasting arms,
That bear us o'er all ill and harms;
For blessed words of long ago
That help us now Thy will to know.
  Father in Heaven, we thank Thee. . . .

"How that beautiful nature would transport my soul
and move it to thanksgiving to the Creator; to think
that He has made all that for us!"
St. Elizabeth of the Trinity

THE FERNS AND THE FLAKES
Emma E. Brown, published in
The Poet and the Children, 1882

"Oh, what shall we do
The long winter through?"
The baby ferns cried
When the mother fern died.
The wind whistled bleak,
And the woodland was drear,
And on each baby check
There glistened a tear.

When down from a cloud
Like a flutter of wings,
There came a great cloud
Of tiny white things.
They fell in a heap
Where the baby ferns lay,
And put them to sleep
That bleak stormy day.

Tucked under the snow
In their brown little hoods,
Not a thing will they know—
These babes in the wood—
Till some day in Spring,
When the bobolinks sing,
They will open their eyes
To the bluest of skies.

"The flying sky is dark with running horses."
John Masefield, "Night Is on the Downland"

THE NORTH WIND DOTH BLOW
Mother Goose/Traditional

The North wind doth blow
And we shall have snow,
And what will poor robin do then, poor thing?
He'll sit in a barn and keep himself warm
And hide his head under his wing, poor thing.

The north wind doth blow,
And we shall have snow,
And what will the bee do then, poor thing?
In his hive he will stay,
'Til the cold's passed away,
And then he'll come out in the spring, poor thing!

The north wind doth blow,
And we shall have snow,
And what will the dormouse do then, poor thing?
Rolled up in a ball,
In his nest snug and small,
He'll sleep 'til warm weather comes in, poor thing!

"Saint Thomas Aquinas wisely noted that multiplicity and variety 'come from the intention of the first agent' who willed that 'what was wanting to one in the representation of the divine goodness might be supplied by another', inasmuch as God's goodness 'could not be represented fittingly by any one creature.'" – *Laudato Si'* 86

HOLY DAYS AND HOLIDAYS

Labor Day
First Monday in September

THEY WHO TREAD THE PATH OF LABOR
(ADAPTED FROM "THE TOILING OF FELIX")
Henry Van Dyke (1852-1933), published in
The Poems of Henry Van Dyke, 1913

They who tread the path of labor
Follow where My feet have trod;
They who work without complaining,
Do the holy will of God;
Nevermore do you need seek me;
I am with you everywhere;
Raise the stone, and you shall find Me,
Cleave* the wood and I am there.

Where the many toil together,
There am I among My own;
Where the tired workman sleeps,
There am I with him alone:
I, the Peace that passes knowledge,
Dwell amid the daily strife;
I, the Bread of Heav'n, am broken
In the sacrament of life.

Every task, however simple,
Sets the soul that does it free;
Every deed of love and mercy,
Done to man is done to Me.
Nevermore do you need seek me;
I am with you everywhere;
Raise the stone, and you shall find Me;
Cleave the wood, and I am there.

* Cut, slice, hew

COME UNTO ME
(MATTHEW 11:28)
Annie Johnson Flint (1866-1932)

Come unto Me, all ye that labor,
That sink beneath your load of care;
Come unto Me when shadows gather,
And raise your hearts to Me in prayer.
I wait to give your souls a blessing,
To lift you upward to My breast;
Come, weary, worn, and heavy-laden,
And I will give you rest. . . .

November 11
Veterans' Day (Armistice Day)

A NATION'S STRENGTH
(Veteran's Day is traditionally celebrated
on November 11 unless this falls on a weekend.)

Ralph Waldo Emerson (1803-1882), published in *Our
Little Kings and Queens at Home and at School,* 1891

What makes a nation's pillars high
And its foundations strong?
What makes it mighty to defy
The foes that round it throng?

It is not gold. Its kingdoms grand
Go down in battle shock;
Its shafts are laid on sinking sand,
Not on abiding rock.

Is it the sword? Ask the red dust
Of empires passed away;
The blood has turned their stones to rust,
Their glory to decay.

And is it pride? Ah, that bright crown
Has seemed to nations sweet;
But God has struck its luster down
In ashes at his feet.

Not gold but only men can make
A people great and strong;
Men who for truth and honor's sake
Stand fast and suffer long.

Brave men who work while others sleep,
Who dare while others fly . . .
They build a nation's pillars deep
And lift them to the sky.

CHRIST, OUR KING

Sister Maryanna Childs, O.P. (1910-19??), published in
A Lovely Gate Set Wide, 1946 [This poem was arranged
to be sung to the tune of "America the Beautiful."]

Hail, King of Kings! Hail, Prince of Peace!
    Our Eucharistic Lord!
In heaven served by angel hosts;
    On earth by men adored.
O Christ, our King, here caroling
    We pledge our youth to Thee.
Great King Divine, our hearts are Thine
    In loving fealty*.

Thy throne is in the starry skies;
    Thou rulest over all,
Yet on each altar dost abide
    To hear Thy children call.
And Thou wilt deign** to live and reign
    In hearts that stainless be;
So keep us pure, help us endure
    In lasting loyalty.

* loyalty

** see fit; consent

A THRONE FOR MY KING

Sister Mary Josita Belger (1899-1978), published in
Sing a Song of Holy Things, 1945

I've build a throne within my heart,
For Jesus is my King.
And when He comes I'll give to Him
My life and everything.

He made the mighty mountains,
The vales and deep blue seas.
But the hearts of little children
Are greater far than these.

The throne within my little heart
I know will please Him more
Than all the gifts of all the lands
That stretch from shore to shore.

I'll keep my heart all swept and clean,
As throne-rooms ought to be.
Then Jesus will be glad to come,
To make His home with me.

First Friday and
First Saturday
Meditations

THE LITTLE MAN

Fr. Leonard Feeney (1897-1978), published in
Gospel Rhymes, 1947

A small little fellow Zacheus was,
   He was maybe not five feet high;
And he climbed up into a sycamore tree
   To watch Our Lord go by.

He tucked up his tunic, and up he crawled
   And was perched on a shady limb,
Where he thought, of course, he was perfectly safe,
   And that no one would notice him.

But Our Lord looked up the minute He came
   To the foot of the sycamore tree,
And He smiled when He saw Zacheus and said:
   "Zacheus, come down to me!"

And everyone murmured and told Our Lord:
   "This man is a dreadful sinner."
But Our Lord said, "Nevertheless, today
   I shall go to his house for dinner."

And down the road to Zacheus's house
   Our Lord and Zacheus went;
And the poor little sinner was deeply touched,
   And he would not be content

Till he had presented his Royal Guest
   With the best that he could afford;
And half of his riches he gave to the poor
   To show that he loved Our Lord.

STONES

T. V. Nicholas, published in *Gospel Rhymes*, 1947

... Three women to the Sepulchre
Their fragrant spices bore
And wondered how to move the stone
That stood across the door.
But when they reached the Sepulchre
The stone they feared was gone,
An angel's hand had pushed it by
And this was Easter morn.

Lord, help me that the stones of life
My trust in you may prove,
You'd never, nerve leave Your friends
With stones they couldn't remove.

132

A CHILD'S GOOD-NIGHT
Published in *Religious Poems for Little Folks*, 1936

Dear Lord, my eyes are full of sleep,
So long has been the day;
And I have given up my toys,
For I am tired of play.

Now when I seek my little bed
I come in haste to Thee.
Good-night, dear Sacred Heart, good-night,
And watch Thou over me.

I know I need Thee always near;
So keep me in Thy sight
Until I come to Thee again,
Dear Sacred Heart, good-night.

OUR LADY'S ASSUMPTION
[ADAPTED]
Hyacinth Blocker (1904-1969), published in
Locust Bloom and Other Poems, 1938

D ear Mother . . .

It was your captivating chastity
That drew the Lord from Heaven's throne to thee.
Ah Mary, only you could call Him down
To earth and give Him birth in Bethlehem's town.

Then surely, Mother, it seems only just
Your body should escape defilement's dust.
No wonder that your Son's own Cherubim
Came down and took you spotless back to Him!

First Friday Devotion Promise #12

"I promise you, in the excessive mercy of my heart that my all-powerful love will grant to all those who receive Holy Communion on the first Friday for nine consecutive months the grace of final repentance; they shall not die in My disgrace nor without receiving the sacraments; My Divine Heart shall be their safe refuge in that last moment."

THERE BLEW A HORN IN BETHLEHEM

Helen Parry Eden (1872-1898), published in
Blackfriars, Volume 8, 1927

There blew a horn in Bethlehem,
Christ sat on Mary's knee,
"And O," she said, "My Child," she said,
"They blow that horn for Thee.
For Thou shall hunt the heart of man,
Thy prey, from hole to hole—
Till at the last Thy little hands
Shall close upon his soul."

135

THE HAIL MARY

Marigold Hunt (1905-1994), published in
Gospel Rhymes, 1947

When Our Lord was a little new baby
And lay on Our Lady's knees,
He heard the bees in the clover,
He heard the wind in the trees.

He remembered making the clover,
And telling the wind to blow,
He remembered putting the hum in a bee
And setting the trees to grow.

He remembered making Our Lady
To be Queen of Everything,
The Crown of the World, and his mother,
He her son and her king—

> The angels call her holy,
> And we will do the same,
> "Holy Mary, Mother of God,"
> Our Lord made her name.

ADDITIONAL RESOURCES

A BOOK
(FROM "LIFE", POEM 21)

Emily Elizabeth Dickinson (1830-1886), published in
The Poetry of Emily Dickinson: Series One, 1896

He ate and drank the precious words,
His spirit grew robust;
He knew no more that he was poor,
Nor that his frame was dust.
He danced along the dingy days,
And this bequest of wings
Was but a book. What liberty
A loosened spirit brings!

Recommended Autumn Picture Books

Stellar Choices

★Appelt, Kathi. *Miss Lady Bird's Wildflowers: How a First Lady Changed America* – In this engaging picture biography, we learn how one woman's love of wildflowers changed the landscape of American highways. How can you share your love of a certain aspect of God's creation to enrich someone else's life?

★Goble, Paul. *Song of Creation* – God is praised by all creation as set forth in Daniel 3:56-88, with winsome illustrations.

★Johnston, Tony. *Winter Is Coming* – In this exquisitely illustrated book, a little girl, nature journal in hand, observes the signs of the approaching winter throughout the months of September, October, and November.

★Lionni, Leo. *Frederick* – Through Frederick—the mouse who gathers more than corn, seeds, and nuts as winter approaches—we learn that we need more than food to sustain us in hard times.

★Wood, Douglas. *Grandad's Prayers of the Earth* – Sharing special times with his grandfather in the woods, a young boy grows in his perception and understanding of the natural world and in his concept of the definition and purpose of prayers.

Holiday and Religious Books

Child, Lydia Maria. *Over the River and through the Wood* – This traditional Thanksgiving poem, first published in

Flowers for Children in 1844, has been set to music and published in numerous picture books with various illustrators. This is a nice one.

Demi. *Mary* – This is an elegant and golden picture book of the Blessed Virgin.

dePaola, Tomie. *Francis: The Song of Francis* – Francis praises God by singing; the angels and birds join in.

Gauch, Patricia Lee. *The Little Friar Who Flew* – Illustrated by Tomie de Paola, this story is of St. Joseph of Copertino (1602-1663), whose feast day is celebrated on September 18.

Lathrop, Dorothy P. *Animals of the Bible* – This older book gives us stories of animals from both the Old and New Testaments with ink drawings that are absolutely worthy of a Caldecott Medal.

Mayer, Marianna. *The Twelve Apostles* – An introduction to Jesus' closest companions with classical paintings as illustrations.

Raven, Margot Theis. *America's White Table* – Perhaps this Veteran's Day, your family can begin a new family tradition with this ceremony of remembrance for our POWs, MIAs, and fallen veterans.

Tickle, Phyllis. *This Is What I Pray Today: The Divine Hours Prayers for Children* – Gentle and sweet prayers based upon the Psalms are presented for each day of the week for morning, rest time, and evening.

Tudor, Tasha. *Time to Keep* – An old-fashioned journey through the year's holidays

Wood, Douglas. *The Secret of Saying Thanks* – With graceful, poetical text and reflective illustrations, we learn the secret to giving thanks—and the secret to happiness.

RESPECTING GOD'S CREATION
(ECO-CATHOLIC)

Aliki. *The Story of Johnny Appleseed* – A simple retelling of the life of John Chapman, this book is graced with oil pastel illustrations.

Burleigh, Robert. *A Man Named Thoreau* – A short biography with black and white drawings

Cherry, Lynne. *The Great Kapok Tree: A Tale of the Amazon Rain Forest* – Learn about the importance of the trees of the forest through this conservation message accompanied with rich, bright illustrations.

dePaola, Tomie. *Let the Whole Earth Sing Praise* – All creation sings praise to God in this joyful book.

Ehrlich, Amy. *Rachel: The Story of Rachel Carson* – This book provides an insightful view into the life of this environmentalist for older readers.

Fleming, Denise. *Where Once There Was a Wood* – This ecological book teaches us how to create wildlife habitats in our neighborhoods.

George, Jean. *The Eagles Are Back* – Colorfully illustrated, this tale tells of a young boy who assists a ranger by watching over an eagle's nest at a time when the eagles are near extinction.

George, Jean. *The Wolves Are Back* – Find out how returning the wolves to Yellowstone National Park restored a better balance of nature there.

Glaser, Linda. *Our Big Home* – A poetic portrayal of the earth we share together as our home

Kerley, Barbara. *A Home for Mr. Emerson* – Informative and interesting, Ralph Waldo Emerson's life is depicted with vivid pictures and quotes from the man himself.

Lasky, Kathryn. *John Muir: America's First Environmentalist* – With gorgeous watercolors and excerpts from John Muir's diary, this short but inspiring biography portrays his love of nature and the role he played in establishing our country's national parks.

Lindbergh, Reeve. *The Circle of Days* – Bright, collaged paintings adorn this canticle of St. Francis, which has been set to rhyme to help us appreciate and give thanks for the beauty of the world around us.

London, Jonathan. *Giving Thanks* – In the spirit of St. Francis and the Native Americans, a boy and his father hike through the fields and forest offering thanks for the gifts of nature.

McLeod, Elaine. *Lessons from Mother Earth* – With poetic text and gentle watercolor illustrations, this book teaches us about foraging in nature's garden.

Okimoto, Jean Davies. *Winston of Churchill* – In this humorous book, we find a polar bear of northern Canada organizing a protest against the melting of the polar ice cap.

Paul, Miranda. *One Plastic Bag: Isatou Ceesay and the Recycling Women of the Gambia* – For older readers, this true story shows how a small action by one person can have a large environmental impact.

Schaefer, Lola M. and Adam. *Because of an Acorn* – The sparse text and colorful illustrations bring home to young children the simple message that all of nature is connected.

Seuss, Dr. *The Lorax* –In this silly, rhyming environmental book with a powerful message, the Once-ler
describes the cause, and possible cure, for the local
pollution problem.

Smith, David J. *If the World Were a Village: A Book
about the World's People* – Instead of looking at the 6.5
billion people in the world as a whole, this book breaks
down the population—by nationality, language, age,
religion, food, air and water, schooling and literacy,
money and possessions, and electricity—so we can see
where we all fit in. By learning "world-mindedness," we
are in a better position to care for our planet.

Van Allsburg, Chris. *Just a Dream* – With small steps
and sacrifices we can take now, we can preserve the
earth for the future.

Wood, Douglas. *Old Turtle* – This book conveys a quiet
message of the interconnection of all creation and how
we can experience more of God by studying nature.

Yolen, Jane. *Johnny Appleseed* – Learn both the facts
and the legends in this interesting and well-formatted
book.

Yolen, Jane. *Mother Earth, Father Sky: Poems about
Our Planet* – A poetic cry for our fragile earth, this collection of 35 poems includes poets such as C.S. Lewis
and Christina Rossetti.

REFLECTING ON THE MYSTERY OF GOD (MYSTIC)

Baylor, Byrd. *Your Own Best Secret Place* – Ever think
that someone else in the past may have used your best

secret place before you? How would it feel to share your own secret place with someone else in the future?

Collins, Pat. *Deer Watch* – A boy and his dad walk and walk to find a deer; it's hard to be quiet in the woods.

Yolen, Jane.. *Nocturne* – Almost a lullaby, this lyrical tribute to nature at night soothes and quiets.

DETECTING GOD IN NATURE
(NATURE DETECTIVE)

Anthony, Joseph. *In a Nutshell* – Through brilliant artwork and engaging text, this book reveals the life of an oak tree—from acorn to tree to soil—and illustrates the cycle of life and the interconnection of all life.

Arnosky, Jim. *Crinkleroot's Nature Almanac* – An interesting walk through the seasons with wildlife signs and activities for each season.

Fleming, Denise. *Time to Sleep* – Winter is coming, and the animals pass the news that it is time to hibernate.

Pak, Kenard. *Goodbye Autumn, Hello* Winter – Two children stroll through their town saying goodbye to the signs of fall and greeting the signs of the approaching winter season.

Rylant, Cynthia. *In November* – In November, animals and people prepare for the coming winter.

Silver, Donald. *One Small Square: Woods* – This lovely series of books covers various habitats. In *Woods*, we are given numerous activities and experiments (with safety tips), a picture field guide, and realistic illustrations to help us encounter and enjoy God's creation.

INSPECTING GOD'S GLORIOUS CREATION (NATURALIST)

Campbell, Sarah C. *Mysterious Patterns: Finding Fractals in Nature* – How are mountains like Queen Anne's Lace? Read the fascinating story of what a mathematician discovered in 1975 through this photographic introduction.

Davies, Nicola. *Bat Loves the Night* – Written on two levels, this informative picture book has realistic illustrations of this diminishing mammal.

Snow, Virginia Brimhall. *Fall Walk* – In short verse, this book illustrates and identifies various autumn leaves. How many of these leaves can you find near your home?

GENERAL NATURE BOOKS

Bardoe, Cheryl. *Gregor Mendel: The Friar Who Grew Peas* – Learn how the world's first geneticist, a Catholic monk, discovered the fundamental aspects of heredity by studying peas.

Berenstain, Stan and Jan. *The Berenstain Bear's Nature Guide* – Papa Bear serves as our guide to nature.

Bruchac, Joseph. *Thirteen Moons on a Turtle's Back* – The story, based upon Native American tradition and illustrated by Thomas Locker, tells of each of the year's thirteen moons.

Fisher, Aileen. *Out in the Dark and Daylight* – With pencil drawings, these 140 poems on nature are grouped according to the seasons.

Florian, Douglas. *Autumnblings* - With many plays on words, these poems are more examples of this poet's romp through the seasons.

Longfellow. (Susan Jeffers). *Hiawatha* – Using excerpts from *The Song of Hiawatha*, the artist illuminates the boyhood of Hiawatha with detailed paintings.

Schnur, Steven. *Autumn: An Alphabet Acrostic* – A short acrostic poem is offered for each letter of the alphabet from the beginning of fall to the chilly start of winter.

Stevenson, Robert L. and Donna Green. *Leaves from a Child's Garden of Verses* – Another nice collection of fifty of Robert Louis Stevenson's poems, this edition is colorfully illustrated.

Worth, Valerie. *All the Small Poems and Fourteen More* – Simple but lyrical nature poems complimented by expressive line drawings for poetry lovers of all ages.

NATURE CHAPTER BOOKS

Below is a short list of excellent nature chapter books to read aloud together. Enjoy!

Birchbark House, The – Louise Erdrich
Bridge to Terabithia – Katherine Paterson
Burgess Animal Book for Children, The – Thornton
    Burgess
Caddie Woodlawn – Carol Ryrie Brink
Complete Tales of Peter Rabbit, The – Beatrix
    Potter
Complete Tales of Winnie the Pooh, The – A. A.
    Milne
Courage of Sarah Noble, The – Alice Dagliesh

Farmer Boy – Laura Ingalls Wilder
Girl of the Limberlost – Gene Stratton Porter
Gone-Away Lake – Elizabeth Enright
Hatchet – Gary Paulsen
Heidi – Johanna Spyri
Miracles on Maple Hill – Virginia Sorensen
Miss Hickory – Carolyn Sherwin Bailey
My Side of the Mountain – Jean Craighead George
Paddle to the Sea – Holling C. Holling
Rascal – Sterling North
Secret Garden, The – Frances Hodgson Burnett
Sign of the Beaver, The – Elizabeth George Speare
Summer of the Monkeys – Wilson Rawls
Swallows and Amazons – Arthur Ransome
Swiss Family Robinson- Johann David Wyss
Where the Red Fern Grows –Wilson Rawls
Wind in the Willows – Kenneth Grahame

RECOMMENDED ADULT RESOURCES

The following lists of books are intended to aid you in becoming more confident as a nature mentor and student of natural history. This subject used to be taught in schools along with reading, writing, and 'rithmetic. In addition, years ago people were more connected to nature through farming, gardening, and general rural living. Scott Sampson states, "By the close of the 1900s, most Americans could describe themselves as naturalists" (*How to Raise a Wild Child*). Browse through the lists and pick at least one book from each category to educate and inspire you. Most books can be found in your local library or purchased new or used online.

The "Why" of Nature

- *Last Child in the Woods: Saving Our Children from Nature-Deficit Disorder* by Richard Louv
- *Step into Nature: Nurturing Imagination and Spirit in Everyday Life* by Patrice Vecchione
- *The Joyful Mystery: Field Notes toward a Green Thomism* by Christopher J. Thompson
- *The Nature Fix: Why Nature Makes Us Happier, Healthier, and More Creative* by Florence Williams

Connection with Nature

- *A Blessing of Toads: A Guide to Living with Nature* by Sharon Lovejoy
- *How to Be a Wildflower: A Field Guide* by Katie Daisy
- *The Curious Nature Guide: Explore the Natural Wonders All Around You* by Clare Walker Leslie
- *The Secret Wisdom of Nature: Trees, Animals, and the Extraordinary Balance of All Living Things* by Peter Wohlleben

📖 *What the Robin Knows: How Birds Reveal the Secrets of the Natural World* by Jon Young

Nature Activity Books—Outdoor Adventuring

📖 *15 Minutes Outside: 365 Ways to Get Out of the House and Connect with Your Kids* by Rebecca P. Cohen [elementary age]

📖 *Go Wild! 101 Things to Do Outdoors before You Grow Up* by Jo Schofield and Fiona Danks [teens]

📖 *Hands-On Nature: Information and Activities for Exploring the Environment with Children* by Jenepher Lingelbach [Grades K-6]

📖 *I Love Dirt: 52 Activities to Help You and Your Kids Discover the Wonders of Nature* by Jennifer Ward [ages 4-8]

📖 *Roots, Shoots, Buckets & Boots: Gardening Together with Children* by Sharon Lovejoy

📖 *Teaching Kids to Love the Earth: Sharing a Sense of Wonder . . . 186 Outdoor Activities for Parents and Other Teachers* by Herman, Passineau, Schimpf, & Treuer [all ages]

📖 *The Boy's Book of Adventure: The Little Guidebook for Smart and Resourceful Boys* by Michele Lecreux [for girls too!]

📖 *The Wild Weather Book: Loads of Things to Do Outdoors in Rain, Wind and Snow* by Fiona Danks and Jo Schofield

📖 *Vitamin N: The Essential Guide to a Nature-Rich Life—500 Ways to Enrich the Health & Happiness of Your Family & Community* by Richard Louv

Nature Journaling

📖 *Drawn to Nature through the Journals of Clare Walker Leslie*

📖 *Keeping a Nature Journal: Discover a Whole New Way of Seeing the World Around You* by Clare Walker Leslie & Charles E. Roth [ideas and "how to"]

📖 *Nature Journal: A Guided Journal for Illustrating and Recording Your Observations of the Natural World* with Clare Walker Leslie

📖 *The Country Diary of an Edwardian Lady* by Edith Holden

📖 *The Naturalist's Notebook for Tracking Changes in the Natural World Around You* by Nathaniel T. Wheelwright & Bernd Heinrich

Nature Crafts and Drawing Books

📖 *Crafting with Nature: Grow or Gather Your Own Supplies for Simple Handmade Crafts, Gifts & Recipes* by Amy Renea

📖 *Make It Wild: 101 Things to Make and Do Outdoors* by Fiona Danks and Jo Schofield

📖 *Nature Crafts for Kids: 50 Fantastic Things to Make with Mother Nature's Help* by Gwen Diehn & Terry Krautwurst

📖 *Peggy Dean's Guide to Nature Drawing and Watercolor: Learn to Sketch, Ink, and Paint Flowers, Plants, Trees, and Animals* by Peggy Dean

Nature Books for Grandparents

📖 *Granny Camp by Sharon Lovejoy*

📖 *The Rhythm of Family: Discovering a Sense of Wonder through the Seasons* by Amanda Blake Soule with Stephen Soule

📖 *Toad Cottages & Shooting Stars: Grandma's Bag of Tricks* by Sharon Lovejoy

The Practice of *Shinrin-yoku:* Forest Therapy or Forest Bathing
- 📖 *Your Guide to Forest Bathing: Experience the Healing Power of Nature* by M. Amos Clifford
- 📖 Review the teaching philosophies of educators such as Maria Montessori and Charlotte Mason

The Practice of Mindfulness
- 📖 *A Catholic Guide to Mindfulness* by Susan Brinkmann, OCDS
- 📖 *The Mindful Catholic: Finding God One Moment at a Time* by Dr Gregory Bottaro
- 📖 *The Practice of the Presence of God* by Br. Lawrence of the Resurrection
- 📖 *The Sacrament of the Present Moment* by Jean-Pierre de Caussade (also published as *Abandonment to Divine Providence*)

"For if they so far succeeded in
knowledge that they could
speculate about the world,
how did they not more
quickly find its Lord?"

Wisdom 13:9

APPENDIX

SEEKING GOD IN NATURE WITH THE CHURCH

ASSURANCES AND GENERAL COUNSELS: SEEKING GOD IN NATURE VS. NATURE WORSHIP

With the advent of the New Age Movement or New Age Spirituality, many Catholics have become rightfully cautious regarding seeking God (and praying with Him) in nature as this book series promotes. In order to re-assure you and provide some general counsel and advice, the following "lessons" are provided regarding the proper place the reverence of God has in His creation and the appropriateness of communing with Him in the natural world. Below are various appropriate passages from the *Catechism of the Catholic Church*, papal documents, and teachings of the United States bishops. By following the guidelines established with these various Church authorities, we can be assured not to go astray or to lead others down a questionable path of holiness.

Remember these basic principles when using the natural world to converse with God and advance in the life of prayer:

1. God is distinct from His creation. A tree is not God, but can help us better understand the attributes, love, and mercy of God.
2. While it is our intent to learn more about the natural world, this knowledge is for the sole purpose of uniting ourselves closer to the living God, the God of all creation.
3. There is nothing that exists that was not created by God—with a purpose. By understanding the uniqueness of each individual creation, its God-given purpose, and its connection to the rest of

creation, we can learn much about God and our relationship with Him and His creation.

4. God wants you to be surrounded with truth, beauty, and goodness. Creation gives us a glimpse of these features of God and fills us with gratitude.

5. The sole purpose of our existence is to unite our will perfectly with the Will of God and so attain perfect happiness in heaven. Any thing, any person, or any "method" or means of prayer that impedes our goal of uniting ourselves with the Triune God by increasing our self-centeredness or deflecting the reverence that belongs to God to any other person or object is not in accordance with divine teaching or the authority of the Catholic Church.

I promote communing with God in the natural world as it has worked unfailingly for me throughout my life— even as a professed Secular Carmelite. God speaks in eternal silence and in holy silence must be heard by the soul. This silence is often found in the stillness of the natural world. Matthew Kelly often speaks of spending time in the "classroom of silence." For me, nature provides the best classroom—free of the distractions of daily life.

If I spend too little time in silence with God in nature, my peace quickly evaporates, just as not frequenting the sacraments or spending too little time with Jesus in the Blessed Sacrament of the Altar does.

What drew me as a convert to the Catholic Church is the Church's vast array of available means to attain holiness. Perhaps this method of communing with the God of the universe will assist you—and your loved ones as well— along the path of holiness. That is my deep desire.

A BRIEF LESSON ON NEW AGE SPIRITUALITY

While the gamut of New Age spirituality is vast and is composed of a variety of theologies, consider the following generally accepted principles of this philosophy: (Note that all of these are in conflict with the teachings of the Catholic Church.)

- No central authority or teaching, no formal doctrine, or membership
- Contains part of many "isms" such as Pantheism (All things are divine.), Gnosticism (salvation by knowledge), and occultism (knowledge or use of supernatural forces or beings)
- God and creation are one. There is no separation between them.
- Christ is a type of energy, not necessarily an individual being.
- Morality is individually determined—moral relativism
- Influenced by Eastern religions and forms of meditation
- Man is divine and perfected through reincarnation.

For our purposes, remember that God and creation are not one. Creation is a *reflection* of God and can help us come to know Him better. Knowledge of the natural world serves to draw us into closer union with the Creator as we come to see the diversity, beauty, and goodness of nature. We can become more deeply connected to God —and grow in gratitude for His constant presence and many gifts—when we see His hand in the world around us and can pray gratefully to Him in the silence of creation. We can join with all creation to sing praise to the glory of our loving God!

LESSONS FROM THE *CATECHISM OF THE CATHOLIC CHURCH*

The following are excerpts from the *Catechism* regarding God and the natural (visible) world that should assure us that this path of union with God is trustworthy and in full communion with the Holy See:

¶32 . . . As St. Paul says of the Gentiles: For what can be known about God is plain to them, because God has shown it to them. Ever since the creation of the world his invisible nature, namely, his eternal power and deity, has been clearly perceived in the things that have been made (Rom 1:19-20; cf., Acts 14:15, 17; 17:27-28; Wis 13:1-9). And St. Augustine issues this challenge: Question the beauty of the earth, question the beauty of the sea, question the beauty of the air distending and diffusing itself, question the beauty of the sky . . . question all these realities. All respond: "See, we are beautiful." Their beauty is a profession [*confessio*]. These beauties are subject to change. Who made them if not the Beautiful One [Pulcher] who is not subject to change? (St. Augustine, *Sermo* 241, 2: Patrologia Latina 38, 1134)

¶41 All creatures bear a certain resemblance to God, most especially man, created in the image and likeness of God. The manifold perfections of creatures—their truth, their goodness, their beauty all reflect the infinite perfection of God. Consequently we can name God by taking his creatures' perfections as our starting point, "for from the greatness and beauty of created things comes a corresponding perception of their Creator" (Wisdom 13:5).

¶293 Scripture and Tradition never cease to teach and celebrate this fundamental truth: "The world was made for the glory of God" (*Dei Filius*, can. # 5: S 3025). St. Bonaventure explains that God created all things "not to increase his glory, but to show it forth and to communicate it" (St. Bonaventure, *In II Sent.* I, 2, 2, 1), for God has no other reason for creating than his love and goodness: "Creatures came into existence when the key of love opened his hand" (St. Thomas Aquinas, *Sent. II*, prol.). The First Vatican Council explains:

This one, true God, of his own goodness and "almighty power", not for increasing his own beatitude, nor for attaining his perfection, but in order to manifest this perfection through the benefits which he bestows on creatures, with absolute freedom of counsel "and from the beginning of time, made out of nothing both orders of creatures, the spiritual and the corporeal. . ." (13 *Dei Filius* I: DS 3002; cf Lateran Council IV (1215): DS 800.7)

¶294 The glory of God consists in the realization of this manifestation and communication of his goodness, for which the world was created. . . ."

GOD TRANSCENDS CREATION AND IS PRESENT TO IT
¶300 God is infinitely greater than all his works: "You have set your glory above the heavens" (Ps 8:1; cf. Sir 43:28). Indeed, God's "greatness is unsearchable" (Ps 145:3). But because he is the free and sovereign Creator, the first cause of all that exists, God is present to his creatures' inmost being: "In him we live and move and have our being" (Acts 17:28). In the words of St. Augustine, God is "higher than my highest and more inward than my innermost self" (St. Augustine, Conf: 3, 6, 11: PL 32, 688). God upholds and sustains creation.

¶337 God himself created the visible world in all its richness, diversity and order. . . . On the subject of creation, the sacred text teaches the truths revealed by God for our salvation (*Dei Verbum* Cf. 11), permitting us to "recognize the inner nature, the value and the ordering of the whole of creation to the praise of God" (*Lumen Gentium* 36 #2).

¶338 Nothing exists that does not owe its existence to God the Creator. . . .

¶339 Each creature possesses its own particular goodness and perfection. . . . Each of the various creatures, willed in its own being, reflects in its own way a ray of God's infinite wisdom and goodness. Man must therefore respect the particular goodness of every creature, to avoid any disordered use of things which would be in contempt of the Creator and would bring disastrous consequences for human beings and their environment.

¶340 God wills the interdependence of creatures: the sun and the moon, the cedar and the little flower, the eagle and the sparrow: the spectacle of their countless diversities and inequalities tells us that no creature is self-sufficient. Creatures exist only in dependence on each other, to complete each other, in the service of each other.

¶341 The beauty of the universe: the order and harmony of the created world results from the diversity of beings and from the relationships which exist among them. Man discovers them progressively as the laws of nature. They call forth the admiration of scholars. The beauty of creation reflects the infinite beauty of the Creator and ought to inspire the respect and submission of man's intellect and will.

¶344 There is a solidarity among all creatures arising from the fact that all have the same Creator and are all ordered to his glory . . .

¶2416 *Animals* are God's creatures. He surrounds them with his providential care. By their mere existence they bless him and give him glory (Cf. Mt 6:26; Dan 3:79-81). Thus men owe them kindness. We should recall the gentleness with which saints like St. Francis of Assisi or St. Philip Neri treated animals.

LESSONS FROM RECENT PAPAL DOCUMENTS

One of the earliest papal documents to call attention to the environment is Pope Saint Paul VI's 1971 letter, *Octogesima Adveniens*, his reflection on the challenges of the post-industrial society. Here, he calls the environment a "wide-ranging social problem which concerns the entire human family" (¶21). Pope Saint John Paul II again addresses ecological matters in the 1988 *Sollicitudo Socialis (On Social Concern)*; and, in 1990, became the first pope to devote an entire papal document to the environmental issue: "Peace with God the Creator, Peace with All of Creation" (1990)—a document well worth reading. An entire chapter of *The Compendium of the Social Doctrine of the Church* (2004) addresses the topic of "Safeguarding the Environment." This chapter was condensed into "The Ten Commandments for the Environment" by Bishop Giampaolo Crepaldi in 2005.

Pope Benedict XVI spent so much of his papacy promoting an environmental message through addresses, encyclicals, and scientific conferences that he became known as the "Green Pope." Pope Francis has spoken frequently about ecological concerns and addressed his 2015 encyclical *Laudato Si': On Care for Our Common*

Home not just to a Catholic audience but to "every person living on this planet" (¶3).

For our purposes, however, let us limit our study to those papal references that especially address seeking and praising God in creation.

"PEACE WITH GOD THE CREATOR, PEACE WITH ALL OF CREATION" (Pope Saint John Paul II, 1990):

¶13 An education in ecological responsibility is urgent . . . The first educator, however, is the family, where the child learns to respect his neighbor and to love nature.

¶14 Finally, the aesthetic value of creation cannot be overlooked. Our very contact with nature has a deep restorative power; contemplation of its magnificence imparts peace and serenity. The Bible speaks again and again of the goodness and beauty of creation, which is called to glorify God . . .

¶16 It is my hope that the inspiration of Saint Francis will help us to keep ever alive a sense of "fraternity" with all those good and beautiful things which Almighty God has created. And may he remind us of our serious obligation to respect and watch over them with care, in light of that greater and higher fraternity that exists within the human family.

COMPENDIUM OF THE SOCIAL DOCTRINE OF THE CHURCH (2004):

¶487 The attitude that must characterize the way man acts in relation to creation is essentially one of gratitude and appreciation; the world, in fact, reveals the mystery of God who created and sustains it. If the relationship with God is placed aside, nature is stripped of its profound meaning and impoverished. If on the other hand,

nature is rediscovered in its creaturely dimension, channels of communication with it can be established, its rich and symbolic meaning can be understood, allowing us to enter into its realm of *mystery*. This realm opens the path of man to God, Creator of heaven and earth. *The world presents itself before man's eyes as evidence of God*, the place where his creative, providential and redemptive power unfolds.

CARITAS IN VERITATE (Pope Benedict XVI, 2009): ¶48 ". . . Nature speaks to us of the Creator (cf. Romans 1:20) and his love for humanity."

MEETING WITH PRIESTS AND DEACONS—August 6, 2008, Pope Benedict XVI: "If we observe what came into being around monasteries, how in those places small paradises, oases of creation were and continue to be born, it becomes evident that these were not only words. Rather, wherever the Creator's Word was properly understood, wherever life was lived with the redeeming Creator, people strove to save creation and not to destroy it."

LAUDATO SI' (Pope Francis, 2015):

¶85 "From panoramic vistas to the tiniest living form, nature is a constant source of wonder and awe. It is also a continuing revelation of the divine." . . . "To sense each creature singing the hymn of its existence is to live joyfully in God's love and hope." This contemplation of creation allows us to discover in each thing a teaching which God wishes to hand on to us, "for the believer, to contemplate creation is the hear a message, to listen to a paradoxical and silent voice."

¶87 When we can see God reflected in all that exists, our hearts are moved to praise the Lord for all his creatures and to worship him in union with them.

¶97 As he [Jesus] made his way throughout the land, he often stopped to contemplate the beauty sown by his Father, and invited his disciples to perceive a divine message in things . . .

¶233 The universe unfolds in God, who fills it completely. Hence, there is a mystical meaning to be found in a leaf, in a mountain trail, in a dewdrop, in a poor person's face. The ideal is not only to pass from the exterior to the interior to discover the action of God in the soul, but also to discover God in all things.

¶234 ". . . the mystic experiences the intimate connection between God and all beings, and thus feels that all things are God." Standing awestruck before a mountain, he or she cannot separate this experience from God, and perceives that the interior awe being lived has to be entrusted to the Lord . . .

¶246 . . . Teach us to discover the worth of each thing, to be filled with awe and contemplation, to recognize that we are profoundly united with every creature as we journey towards your infinite light.

Lessons from the United States Conference of Catholic Bishops

In 1991, the United States Conference of Catholic Bishops published *Renewing the Earth: An Invitation to Reflection and Action on Environment in Light of Catholic Social Teaching*, and, in 2001, *Global Climate Change: A Plea for Dialogue, Prudence, and the Common Good*. Let us examine some excerpts from the former document.

For many people, the environmental movement has reawakened appreciation of the truth that, through the created gifts of nature, men and women encounter their

Creator. The Christian vision of a sacramental universe —a world that discloses the Creator's presence by visible and tangible signs—can contribute to making the earth a home for the human family once again. Pope John Paul II has called for Christians to respect and protect the environment, so that through nature people can "contemplate the mystery of the greatness and love of God. . . . Dwelling in the presence of God, we begin to experience ourselves as part of creation, as stewards within it, not separate from it. As faithful stewards, full-ness of life comes from living responsibly within God's creation (III-A).

Nature shares in God's goodness, and contemplation of its beauty and richness raised our hearts and minds to God. . . . Through the centuries, Catholic theologians and philosophers, like St. Paul before them, continue to search for God in reasoning about the created world (IV-A).

We remind *parents* that they are the first and principal teachers of children. It is from parents that children will learn love of the earth and delight in nature. It is at home that they develop the habits of self-control, concern, and care that lie at the heart of environmental morality (V-B).

TWO CURRENT PRACTICES

Seeking God and communing with Him in nature raises several potential "red flags" regarding two currently pop-ular practices: the Japanese practice of *shinrin-yoku*, or forest therapy (forest bathing) and mindfulness.

Many scientific studies show that spending time in nature can have a positive effect on us physically, emotionally, and spiritually. Forest therapy, a concept practiced in-stinctively for eons, has fallen from practice in modern times. Spending refreshing periods of time with God in the natural world can be spiritually empowering. Organized "immersions" are becoming popular. Be cautious and aware, ensuring that the focus centers on God the Creator—source of all existence.

Mindfulness, derived from a Buddhist meditation technique, also has the potential to lead a Catholic astray. Although similar to the accepted Catholic practices of the Practice of the Presence of God and the Sacrament of the Present Moment, Buddhist mindfulness is centered on the mind; Catholic meditation always centers on God. We want to treasure each moment with God in the natural world, but only in a way that leads us directly to Him.

Educate yourself regarding these two practices by reading one or more of the resources suggested in the Appendix, or research these practices online.

———————

As we deepen our connection with nature—and therefore with our loving God—let us try to develop a "sacramental imagination." According to Mary C. Boys, this is a "vision that sees all creation as mediating the divine." This vision may be easier for children than adults. To seek God through His creation, search for His reflection —consider what each creation can teach us about God, and embrace each gift of nature as a continuation of the mystery that is God: "Even when he reveals himself, God remains a mystery beyond words: 'If you understood him, it would not be God'" *(CCC* ¶230 quoting St. Augustine).

Immerse yourself in nature. Ponder in holy silence His wondrous creation. In all things, give Him glory. Give thanks.